D0862523

WISDOM FOR EVERYDAY LIFE
FROM THE BOOK OF REVELATION

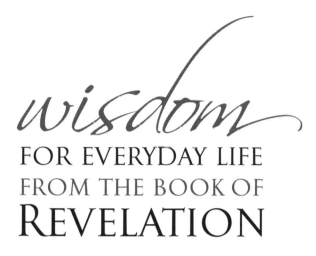

wisdom

FOR EVERYDAY LIFE
FROM THE BOOK OF
REVELATION

FR. RICHARD VERAS

SERVANT
BOOKS

PUBLISHED BY ST. ANTHONY MESSENGER PRESS
CINCINNATI, OHIO

RESCRIPT

In accord with the *Code of Canon Law*, I hereby grant my permission to publish *Wisdom for Everyday Life From the Book of Revelation.*

Reverend Joseph R. Binzer

Vicar General

Archdiocese of Cincinnati

Cincinnati, Ohio

October 15, 2009

Permission to publish is a declaration that a book or pamphlet is considered to be free of doctrinal or moral error. It is not implied that those who have granted the permission to publish agree with the contents, opinions or statements expressed.

Unless otherwise noted, Scripture passages have been taken from the *Revised Standard Version,* Catholic edition. Copyright 1946, 1952, 1971 by the Division of Christian Education of the National Council of Churches of Christ in the USA. Used by permission. All rights reserved.

Note: The editors of this volume have made minor changes in capitalization to some of the Scripture quotations herein. Please consult the original source for proper capitalization.

Cover and book design by Mark Sullivan

Cover image © Martin Ruegner / Radius Images / Veer

LIBRARY OF CONGRESS CATALOGING-IN-PUBLICATION DATA

Veras, Richard.

Wisdom for everyday life from the book of Revelation / Richard Veras.

p. cm.

Includes bibliographical references and index.

ISBN 978-0-86716-905-8 (pbk. : alk. paper) 1. Bible. N.T. Revelation—Commentaries. 2. Bible. N.T. Revelation—Criticism, interpretation, etc. I. Title.

BS2825.53.V47 2010

223'.8077—dc22

2009038045

ISBN 978-0-86716-905-8

Published by Servant Books, an imprint of St. Anthony Messenger Press.

28 W. Liberty St.

Cincinnati, OH 45202

www.ServantBooks.org

Printed in the United States of America.

Printed on acid-free paper.

10 11 12 13 14   5 4 3 2 1

Introduction   • *vii*

Chapter One   *The Vision of Jesus and the Letters to*
                     the Churches: Seeing the Lord Who
                     Was Already There, Revelation 1—3   • *1*

Chapter Two   *The Throne of the Three, the*
                     Proclamation of the Four, and the
                     Worship of the Twenty-Four,
                     Revelation 4—5   • *16*

Chapter Three *The Seven Seals: Jesus Is Present in the*
                     Mess of History, Revelation 6—7   • *29*

Chapter Four   *The Old and the New: The Plagues, the*
                     Two Witnesses, the Ark of the Covenant,
                     and the Woman, Revelation 8—12   • *44*

Chapter Five   *Devilish Imitations,* Revelation 13   • *64*

Chapter Six   *Love Versus Power,* Revelation 13—16   • *75*

Chapter Seven *Babylon the Harlot and Jerusalem the*
                     Bride, Revelation 17—18; 12; 21   • *89*

Chapter Eight   *The Final Victory: The Marriage*
                     of Jesus and His Church,
                     Revelation 19—21   • *100*

Epilogue   *Come, Lord Jesus!*   • *124*

Notes   • *127*

•

•

•

•

•

I used to teach religion in an all-boys Catholic high school, and the curriculum of sophomore year was the New Testament. In May and June, as the school year was drawing to a close and classrooms were hot and attention spans evaporating, the book of Revelation was a gift of God's mercy to a poor teacher trying to get teenage boys to pay attention to Scripture. Battles and dragons and monsters from the deep gave my students and me a second wind to carry us through to the academic finish.

You learn any subject better when you have to teach it, and having to communicate the truths of the book of Revelation to my students gave me a greater appreciation of this strange account at the end of the Bible. Much more than a curiosity to close the year, I discovered it to be a catechesis that summarizes foundational truths of Christianity. It became an excellent review of what I had spent the year trying to teach my students about Jesus.

Apocalyptic Literature: Our Ultimate Destiny Seen in Symbols
The book of Revelation is written in the style of apocalyptic literature. In fact, it is sometimes referred to as simply "the Apocalypse," which comes from the Greek word *apokalypsis*, which means "revelation." This style of writing was also

employed by the Jews, as evidenced by the book of Daniel in the Old Testament.

One characteristic of apocalyptic literature is that it emphasizes the end times, the culmination of history. However, it is important to note that our ultimate destiny has everything to do with our life in the present. The Church would not have included the book of Revelation in the New Testament canon if the book did not have something to say about the Christian life we live here and now. That the Church sets this book before us as inspired Scripture tells us that it has relevance for every Christian in every historical moment and circumstance. The battle it speaks about is a universal battle, so it refers in some way to every battle, great and small, that is fought in the Church's pilgrimage through time.

The most immediately obvious characteristic of apocalyptic literature is that it is written in symbolic language. Indeed, the relentless use of strange symbolism in the book of Revelation is what makes it daunting to many. (It is also what makes it rather enticing to certain personality types. I know two teenage brothers who look forward to family vacations because they can grab the Bible in the hotel room and scare each other by reading random passages.)

As we shall see, much of the symbolism is not so strange when we look at Revelation with an eye to the scriptural tradition that precedes it. Other symbols can be seen more clearly when we consider the historical and political circumstances in which the book was written. This brief look at the book of Revelation will not attempt to explain each and every symbol (thus my young friends' hotel fright nights will not be completely ruined) but will look at the major sections of the book to show what they reveal about Christ and the Church.

Why Symbols?

The question that arises in front of this densely symbolic book is *why?* Why this heavy use of strange imagery? Why did the author not just write clearly what he wanted to communicate? The position you take in response to these questions will largely determine whether reading Revelation will be a trial of your patience or a fascinating exposition of your faith.

Why don't we always just say what we want to say? Have you had the experience of being frustrated with words because they are not expressive enough? How many times does "I love you" fall short? How many times are you at a loss for words to express your wonder, your anger, your disappointment, or your excitement? Often images more adequately express realities we can't explain with words.

I once had the privilege of visiting the Van Gogh Museum in Amsterdam. I am not an art expert, but I found myself moved almost to tears in front of some of his paintings of trees, landscapes, and humble homes. I was astounded that Van Gogh understood a certain sadness I experience when I'm outside at dusk and a certain melancholy that belongs to the autumn.

Music is an aural image, if you will. I have a friend who hates musicals: He claims that the songs only serve to interrupt the plot. I have always liked musicals, and my contrary friend challenged me to help him understand what I like about the musical moments.

You see, the point is not to stop the plot but rather to make *us* stop before a particular moment and consider the meaning behind what is happening. The musical moments show us the true dimensions of the events being told. (Note: This is in a *good* musical; I don't defend the clunkers!) Plots of many musicals have to do with the boy meeting the girl, the boy struggling to get the girl, the boy conquering the girl's heart, and love triumphing over obstacles. But there is much more to it than only that!

A richer example is classical music. Symphonies and concertos have no words or plots at all, and yet this music can call out to the depths of the human heart and touch and almost grasp eternal and universal beauty as perhaps no other genre of music can.

Visual and aural images, symbols, if you will, express the depth of reality more truly than literal descriptions of what the eye can see and the ear can hear. Psalm 49 speaks, or rather sings, of this:

> My mouth shall speak wisdom;
>   the meditation of my heart shall be understanding.
> I will incline my ear to a proverb;
>   I will solve my riddle to the music of the lyre. (Psalm 49:3–4)

The Infinite Dimensions of Life

Our lives could be described as merely one event after another. Basically, every one of us wakes up each day, does things, and goes to bed. But there is more to life than that. There are reasons and meanings behind our gestures.

The book of Revelation seeks to underscore the infinite dimensions behind the encounter with Christ and the decision to follow him. Seemingly banal decisions and events carry meanings that are universal and cataclysmic and that echo unto eternity. Saint Paul recognizes this when he says, "For we are not contending against flesh and blood, but against the principalities, against the powers, against the world rulers of this present darkness, against the spiritual hosts of wickedness in the heavenly places" (Ephesians 6:12).

The infinite importance behind the events of life is not something open only to the religious minded. Everyone has this sense. Look at the popular movies in our own culture.

Two of the most popular film serials are *The Lord of the Rings* and *Star Wars*. In the former you have four hobbits whose actions will rescue Middle Earth; in the latter you have a small group of friends whose actions save the universe. Why are these films so popular? Because all of us would like our own lives and actions to be that consequential, to carry that kind of weight. Why are the *Spiderman* movies hits? Because every nerdy guy would like to be the savior of New York City. *The Princess Diaries*? Because every girl would like to be told she is, in actuality, a princess.

The Fantasticks, the longest running musical in New York history, opens with an ordinary young girl who says, "It's not possible for me to have the feelings I have and be a button maker's daughter!" She conjectures that she must be a princess. I suspect this sense of hidden greatness is universal.

Real-life weddings offer another example. If priests are not careful, they can slip into a very cynical attitude toward weddings, especially priests in urban areas, who might preside over forty or more in a year. You meet with the couple, and they choose the same readings and hymns as hundreds of couples before them. It can be easy to look at them as "couple number whatever." However, this would be a horrible mistake.

The truth is that this wedding is unique, for the couple and the relationship they share are unique. The way they have come to this commitment is particular to their personalities and histories. Their vocation to marriage is original and unrepeatable.

Think of it, with every sacramental marriage the Word becomes flesh in the world in a new way through the particular love shared by that couple. Thus the readings and hymns are there to celebrate and call our attention to infinite dimensions of the event of their marriage. The couple's sense of the importance of their wedding day is much closer to the truth of what is really happening than an outsider's perception. The ceremony may be similar to others, but it marks a singular newness.

The book of Revelation, with all of its symbolism and grandiosity, draws our attention to the fact that following Jesus is a gesture of inestimable worth and incalculable proportion. The life of the Christian is put in the context of the ultimate battle. We are the real hobbits! We are the friends whose lives can bring salvation to the universe! Our victory will bring with it the crown of life, so we will be the *real* heroes and princesses!

But our victory will only come about through communion with Christ. Our victory is the echo of his victory. This communion is not abstract. It is as close as the union of a bride and groom. In fact, the culmination of the victory is depicted as a wedding feast in which the Church is indissolubly united with Christ in a bond that lasts forever. This is why every wedding is so dignified. For every nuptial ceremony makes that ultimate wedding feast somehow present and thus awakens our hearts.

As you read the book of Revelation along with me, my hope is that you will discover Jesus anew and thus discover who you are as one of his disciples. You will be amazed at how important your life really is!

CHAPTER ONE

•

•

•

•

•

The Vision of Jesus and the Letters to the Churches:
Seeing the Lord Who Was Already There
Revelation 1—3

The Revelation is given by Jesus Christ to John. Some Fathers of the Church tell us that this is John the apostle and writer of the fourth Gospel; others tell us that this is another John. It seems likely that if it is not the apostle himself, it is one of his disciples, because the Gospel of John and the book of Revelation share common themes and references.

This John tells us that the revelatory vision occurred when he was exiled on the island of Patmos for preaching Jesus Christ, revealing at the outset that Revelation is written in reference to a time of persecution. Whether it was the persecution of the Roman Emperor Nero, which occurred around the year AD 64, or that of Domitian, which occurred from 92 until 96, can also be argued. Perhaps the original hearers of this book would have recognized certain references to Nero and understood them to be comments about Domitian, much as we might use Hitler to comment on the ferocity of subsequent dictators.

John's Vision of Jesus

So we have an exile named John who is writing to other Christians who, in this time of persecution, risk suffering his same fate or worse. John and his friends feel a great urgency to know that they are not alone, that Christ has not abandoned them in this difficult time.

If we reflect on our own experience, we see that it is in the dark moments of life that we either beg for Christ's presence or experience doubt because he seems absent. It is in these moments that we need a friend to remind us that Christ does not leave us alone and to help us recognize that he is with us. Thus one of the major themes of the book of Revelation is that Jesus Christ is truly present in the midst of his Church. In writing this book John is being a true friend to us.

Interestingly, it is John the apostle who stayed close to Jesus during his hour of persecution; and in his account of the passion, John shows us that Jesus was certain of his Father's presence at every step. In the same way, John's vision in Revelation tells us that we can be certain of Jesus' presence in the midst of our suffering.

What did John see?

I saw seven golden lampstands, and in the midst of the lampstands one like a Son of man, clothed with a long robe and with a golden sash across his chest; his head and his hair were white as white wool, white as snow; his eyes were like a flame of fire, his feet were like burnished bronze, refined as in a furnace, and his voice was like the sound of many waters; in his right hand he held seven stars, from his mouth issued a sharp two-edged sword, and his face was like the sun shining in full strength.

... [He said,] "Fear not, I am the first and the last, and the living one; I died, and behold I am alive for evermore, and I have the keys of Death and Hades." (Revelation 1:12–16, 17–18)

This impressive image of Jesus bears some resemblance to a description of God in chapter seven of the Old Testament book of Daniel, as well as the description of Jesus at the Transfiguration. The fiery eyes of Jesus are the eyes that looked at Peter after his denial, the eyes that looked upon the rich young man with a love greater than that sad man had for himself, the eyes that moved Zacchaeus and the Samaritan woman to follow him because the gaze of Jesus burned through to the very cores of their hardened hearts. The face of Jesus, which shines like the sun, is the face of the one who called himself the light of the world.

The sword coming from Jesus' mouth is the Word of God, which pierces more surely than a two-edged sword (see Hebrews 4:12). Think of his words to the Pharisees when they questioned him about whether to stone the adulteress (John 8:7). They were arguing about religious and civic law, but when Jesus said that he who had no sin should cast the first stone, this cut right to the heart. In an instant their arguments were slashed, and they were faced squarely with their own relationship with God. When Jesus' words cut to the heart, it is in order to have mercy, for it is only from the depth of the heart that a real relationship with Jesus can arise.

The Presence of Jesus Among Us
One of the few times a symbol is explained in Revelation is when Jesus tells John, "As for the mystery of the seven stars which you saw in my right hand, and the seven golden

lampstands, the seven stars are the angels of the seven churches, and the seven lampstands are the seven churches" (Revelation 1:20).

The seven churches are seven particular churches that existed in Asia Minor. However, the number seven for the Jews also meant totality or completion. In Genesis, for instance, God rested on the seventh day when creation was complete. And when Jesus told Peter to forgive seventy times seven times (Matthew 18:22), he didn't mean to give up after 490 offenses but to forgive always. Seven connotes limitlessness.

So in speaking of the seven churches, Jesus is not referring only to those seven churches for whom he will dictate letters, but he is speaking to the entire Church. That he is standing in the midst of the seven lampstands tells us that Jesus stands in the midst of the Church.

It is interesting that John mentions seeing the seven lampstands before he mentions seeing Jesus in their midst. This points to the fact that the ordinary way I encounter Jesus today is through encountering members of his Church. In seeing how they live, I begin to become aware that there is something or someone exceptional among them. Recall that Jesus said, "Where two or three are gathered in my name, there am I in the midst of them" (Matthew 18:20).

That Jesus holds the seven stars in his hands tells us that he has the whole Church in his hands. As Jesus commended himself into his Father's hands at the cross, so the Church is in the hands of Jesus. He is with us, and he holds us; we are not alone.

Jesus' real presence in the Church is also evident when we look at the introductions to the seven letters. For each letter begins with one part of John's initial description of Jesus or, in the case of the last two letters, adds something to the description:

2:1: "The words of him who holds the seven stars in his right hand, who walks among the seven golden lampstands."

2:8: "The first and the last, who died and came to life."

2:12: "Who has the sharp two-edged sword."

2:18: "Who has eyes like a flame of fire, and whose feet are like burnished bronze."

3:1: "Who has the seven spirits of God and the seven stars."

3:7: "Who has the key of David, who opens and no one shall shut, who shuts and no one opens."

3:14: "The Amen, the faithful and true witness, the beginning of God's creation."

When you put the seven introductions together, you get the complete description of Christ. This is a beautiful way of expressing the fact that Christ becomes recognizably present through our unity: That is, the Church united forms the one body of Christ and witnesses to his presence. Recall that in John's Gospel Jesus prayed, "That they may all be one; even as you, Father, are in me, and I in you, that they also may be in us, so that the world may believe that you have sent me" (John 17:21).

John expresses the same reality revealed through Saint Paul's description of the Church as the mystical body of Christ: "As in one body we have many members, and all the members do not have the same function, so we, though many, are one body in Christ, and individually members one of another" (Romans 12:4).

At the very outset John reassures us that Christ is present not only spiritually but physically through the witness given to the world by the men and women who make up his body in the world. If the lampstands are not there to illuminate him, I will not clearly see the Son of God. Without the witnesses of the Church, I am in danger of following the false Christ of my imagination or of someone else's imagination.

Church history presents us with a messy and winding pilgrimage through time, but it is only that history that enables us to see Christ present and active down through the centuries. Likewise it is much easier to follow the spiritual Christ than the one who has chosen to be present to me through that part of the Church in which I find myself. For me this means my family, my friends in the lay movement Communion and Liberation, through which my faith is enlivened, my brother priests, my students, my colleagues, my parishioners, and the publishing company who invited me to write this book! For others it means their spouse, children, parents, and friends, with all the patience these require and the gifts they offer.

As I write this chapter, for instance, it is a snow day, one of the few occasions on which I can have a good chunk of time to write. I am on a roll and would like to stay in my room and commune with my Bible and my computer and enjoy the energy and the inspiration that the Spirit seems to be giving me. Alas, the phone has rung, and my fellow priests want to rough the roads and go out for dinner, rather than stay home and fix ourselves sandwiches. I can decline and remain here, serving Christ through my writing, but it seems strange to do that at the expense of an opportunity of community life, so rarely lived anymore among priests. Christ has bumped into me again through his body, and my yes is a way of begging for his presence and following him.

Jesus did not say that he is present only when two or three are praying or performing some work of service in his name; he said that when two or three are gathered doing anything in his name, he is present. Certainly he is present in the companionship around a meal, and we hope he is present in the midst of three priests as they skid through the streets of New York in search of one.

Letters to the Churches

It is important to note that Christ writes these letters not to individuals but to churches. In Pope Benedict XVI's address to the bishops of the United States, which we could consider a kind of letter to the Church in the United States, he warned of an individualism that can affect the Church, "giving rise to a form of piety which sometimes emphasizes our private relationship with God at the expense of our calling to be members of a redeemed community."[1] In answering the bishops' questions, the pope underlined this point again:

> Christian faith, as we know, is essentially ecclesial, and without a living bond to the community, the individual's faith will never grow to maturity.
>
> …
>
> In Christianity, there can be no room for purely private religion: Christ is the Savior of the world, and, as members of his Body …, we cannot separate our love for him from our commitment to the building up of the Church.… To the extent that religion becomes a purely private affair, it loses its very soul.[2]

A priest I know was acting as spiritual director for a small community of sisters who were going through a difficult moment, and he recognized that a large part of their problem was that they saw their community life as a kind of accident. Their attitude was that Jesus had called each of them individually, and in order to follow this personal call, they had to join this community of other women who had a similar call. The fact that they were in the same house was seen as a circumstance that required them to tolerate each other, as one might put up with a college roommate.

Vocation is certainly a personal call; however, one of the privileged ways that Jesus relates to us is through community. In some way each of those sisters in that community was essential to the other. The priest counseled that if there were a personality conflict or a difficulty, the sister should not perceive it as an obstacle to her relationship with Christ but rather discern what change Christ was asking of her through the relationship with the other sister. Christ invites us to mature through community.

We learn what love is through community. My involvement in the lay movement Communion and Liberation has formed me as a man and as a priest. My involvement in the education of the students I teach each year and my relationships with them are not add-ons to my relationship with Christ but rather essential components of that relationship—because Christ himself has chosen to make it so!

The same could be said for marriage. I remember a young mother in one of the parishes where I worked who was extremely active in a number of organizations. At a parish dinner an enthusiastic matchmaker introduced her to an eligible bachelor in our parish. The young mother was quite embarrassed, and she discreetly informed the meddling parishioner that she was, in fact, married. I can't blame the meddler, because for a long time I too had thought she was a single mom! She was a very good woman who had a great desire for Christ. But if a woman is married sacramentally, her desire for Christ cannot be lived without reference to her relationship with her spouse.

Baptism is the moment when Christ personally takes us to himself and makes us members of his body. To be a member of his body is to be a member of his Church. Godparents are signs that we cannot live the faith alone but must live it in a community. So much is the Christian bound to the community that, in the case of an infant baptism, the parents and godparents make the profession of faith for the child.

Jesus speaks to all the churches in the same way that Benedict XVI speaks to the entire Church in the United States. We are members of one body, we follow Christ in and through our unity, and so we receive the same correction and the same fatherly direction. We are on the road together.

Words of Correction
After the greeting and the reiteration of a piece of John's description of his vision of Jesus, most of the letters contain a correction from Jesus. The correction in the first letter, addressed to Ephesus, may be the basis of every other correction: "You have abandoned the love you had at first" (Revelation 2:4).

If Christianity is not born and continually enlivened by the experience of being loved by Christ, it is going to degenerate into rules that I may or may not follow but will surely come to resent. It will be a meaningless repetition of truths that I may even believe but that have no impact on my life. Sometimes the experience of Christ's love is pathetically approximated with superficial friendliness or sentimentality. I often hear youth retreat leaders tell me that a retreatant was so moved that he or she cried—as if that passing, emotional moment were the pinnacle of Christian experience. But moralism, empty belief, or bursts of sentimentality cannot sustain the human person and cannot sustain the Church.

In his first letter John writes, "In this is love, not that we loved God but that he loved us" (1 John 4:10). If I am not moved by the experience of the love of Christ that comes to me through the flesh of his Church, if I am not attracted to the Christ whose presence I recognize as the core of all that is good in the Church, then the Church becomes like a political party, perhaps even a really good one, and the best that I can be is a good member.

The Christians of Ephesus had labored well, had recognized and rebuked false doctrine, and even had suffered in the name of Jesus without growing weary. Yet they had taken their gaze away from the love that attracted them to Jesus in the first place, and if this was not corrected, their efforts would be lifeless. In his Letter to the Corinthians, Saint Paul says that we can do all kinds of good works, but without love we are a clanging cymbal (see 1 Corinthians 13).

And so this first correction in this first of the seven letters proclaims that it is Christ himself and his love for us that are the life of the Church. This is the love that leads us on our pilgrimage to the Father, the source of all love. In John's Gospel

Jesus tells the disciples, "Abide in my love" (John 15:9). In the end there is no other way for the Church to abide.

This can explain the corrections to the churches in Sardis and Laodicea. Jesus tells Sardis, "You have the name of being alive, and you are dead" (Revelation 3:1).

I remember being on a committee for a Jubilee conference in the year 2000. One committee member was going to call local religious communitics and "pressure" them into coming. The main concern was not to proclaim Christ but to have numbers, to have the "name of being alive."

Jesus tells Laodicea, "I know your works.... Because you are lukewarm, ... I will spew you out of my mouth. For you say, I am rich, I have prospered, and I need nothing; not knowing that you are wretched, pitiable, poor, blind, and naked" (Revelation 3:15–17). Jesus is telling the Laodiceans that they seem not to need his love, but in reality they are infinitely needy, and their hearts are pining for his love.

All of us on that Jubilee committee were deeply in need of an experience of Christ's love, but our gaze was on something else. The conference came and went and left no lasting impression. Our programs and plans and strategies can distract us and numb our need for the love of Christ.

Empty Pursuits

The corrections that Jesus gives to Pergamum and Thyatira refer to other ways we sabotage our heart's desire for him (see Revelation 2:12–29). Both churches are brought to task for eating food sacrificed to idols and for playing the harlot. To eat food sacrificed to idols is to turn from Jesus and bow down before false gods; in fact, it was one of the ways that

Christians under persecution in the Roman Empire would be invited to deny Christ.

Our current American culture has its own ways of inviting us to deny Christ. In his visit to the United States in 2008, Benedict XVI warned us against materialism:

> It is easy to be entranced by the almost unlimited possibilities that science and technology place before us; it is easy to make the mistake of thinking we can obtain by our own efforts the fulfillment of our deepest needs. This is an illusion. Without God, who alone bestows upon us what we by ourselves cannot attain, our lives are ultimately empty.[3]

How many parents send their children to Catholic schools not so that the children can deepen their faith but so that they can be prepared for a good job and make a good amount of money? For how many of us are schools seen as training centers in which students are told they can obtain their deepest desires by their own efforts and perhaps pay lip service to an irrelevant god? How many students are thus being taught to lead lives that will be ultimately empty?

Do we ever think that the true good of the child depends upon mature faith in Jesus Christ? For how many parents is that a real concern? For how many teachers?

As for "playing the harlot," in the same speech Pope Benedict spoke against "the degrading manifestations and the crude manipulation of sexuality so prevalent today."[4] When the teenage boys I taught would speak casually about the sexual activity that our culture has engendered, I could hear in their voices an underlying cynicism regarding love. When a boy gets good at pretending to love a girl in order have sex, he must begin to wonder if real love actually exists or if everyone is just playing games.

The same must happen to the girls for whom these boys pretend. If real love doesn't exist, then all that is left is to cajole and manipulate and attempt to get whatever substitutes one can. Life must become quite lonely. Playing the harlot is not harmless fun; it can harden the heart toward the love of Christ, the love for which we are made.

The prevalence of divorce likewise can sow seeds of cynicism toward love. Here we see an example of a decision that is not merely personal but affects the communities where it happens. As a good and faithful marriage builds up the Church; divorce carries its own ramifications for the community.

"Playing the harlot" is certainly not limited to sexual sins. Any time I place anything before Jesus in my quest for happiness, I am cheating on the one for whom I am made, the one and only Bridegroom of the Church and of every human heart. If my destiny is union with Jesus at the wedding feast of heaven, then the courtship and engagement happen in this life. How often do I, Jesus' betrothed, play the harlot?

Words of Tenderness

Smyrna and Philadelphia are the only two churches that do not receive corrections. They receive instead a tender overture of love. Interestingly, the love letter to Smyrna begins by recognizing that church's poverty, and the letter to Philadelphia begins by recognizing that church's limited strength. Jesus is most tender toward the weakest of the churches, and it is these churches that have remained most faithful to his love.

The very things that we are most ashamed of are the things that lead us to Jesus. That he loves me in my weakness is what makes me marvel at the nature of his love.

I remember seeing a video on priestly vocations in which every priest was portrayed as a kind of self-made superhero. It made me very uncomfortable, because my experience of vocation, indeed my experience of faith, is that Christ has tenderness toward my weaknesses and that it is not my strength but rather my weakness that draws me to him. To deny my own weakness is to deny his expressions of tenderness toward me.

Recall what Jesus said to Saint Paul: "My grace is sufficient for you, for my power is made perfect in weakness" (2 Corinthians 12:9). Paul reflected upon this and concluded, "I will all the more gladly boast of my weaknesses, that the power of Christ may rest upon me. For the sake of Christ, then, I am content with weaknesses, insults, hardships, persecutions, and calamities; for when I am weak, then I am strong" (2 Corinthians 12:9–10).

"Christ's power is made perfect in weakness." This could be the battle cry for the great struggle that is going to ensue. For all seven letters to the churches end with a hint of an inevitable battle in which no one will be spared a role. Jesus ends each message by promising the gifts that will be given to the one who wins the victory. This battle is a major theme of the book of Revelation.

As in *The Lord of the Rings* and *Star Wars*, there will be many important scenes of the battle that do not directly involve combat, but the struggle is always looming, and the climax is longingly awaited. The churches that are most battle-ready are those that have the least strength, for the victor will not be the one who relies on his own power but the one who entrusts himself completely to the love of Jesus Christ and who accepts his tender pity. The theme of all of the letters of preparation can be summed up in the words of Jesus at the Last Supper, "Apart from me you can do nothing" (John 15:5).

CHAPTER TWO

•

•

•

•

•

The Throne of the Three, the Proclamation of the Four, and the Worship of the Twenty-Four
Revelation 4—5

At the end of the letters to the seven churches, we get an abrupt and magnificent scene change: It is as when a movie quickly goes from a dark indoor or evening scene to one of bright daylight. Our eyes take a moment to adjust. We are in heaven! And John's description of heaven is quite strange but quite revelatory.

In the fantastical Woody Allen film *The Purple Rose of Cairo,* a character from a movie walks out of the screen and is introduced to reality by a poor working girl. (He knows nothing but what is in the plot of his movie.) When she brings him into a church and describes it as the place of God, he asks who God is. After a moment of shock she replies, "God? He's the reason for everything!"

In John's "movie," which we call Revelation, he begins his description of heaven with the One who is clearly the reason for everything that is happening around him.

The Unity of the Trinity

The One on the throne is surrounded by twenty-four elders, perhaps representing the twelve tribes of Israel and the twelve apostles. We are told that seven torches of fire burn before the throne and that these are the seven spirits of God.

Recall now the significance of the number seven: It means fullness or completion. Thus, these seven spirits of God are the way that John describes the one Spirit of God, which we call the Holy Spirit. He is represented by fire, just as at Pentecost he descended upon the apostles in tongues of fire.

Since God's seven spirits are distinguished from the One on the throne, it would seem that John's vision as described thus far is of the Father and the Spirit. Where is the Son?

Interestingly, after describing the seven spirits, John tells us about the four living creatures. These creatures are first mentioned in the apocalyptic vision of Ezekiel in the Old Testament. The Church has come to see them as images of the four Gospels. One has the face of a lion (Mark, who begins his Gospel with John the Baptist crying out like a lion in the desert), another an ox (Luke, who begins with a sacrifice in the temple—an ox was an animal of sacrifice), another a human being (Matthew, who begins with a genealogy of Jesus' human origins), and one an eagle (John, who begins by telling us that Jesus is God descended to earth, and whose theology and familiarity with Jesus seem to soar above the other Gospels).

These creatures are both in the midst of the throne *and* around the throne. This might be an interesting hint at the presence of Jesus. We stand for the Gospel reading at Mass because Jesus is made present in the Gospel. The four living

17

creatures are somehow the link between God who is on the throne and those who are around the throne worshiping, as Jesus himself is for us the face of the Father and the way to the Father. They constantly proclaim the holiness of God, which is what Jesus constantly does.

However, the four creatures are only a hint at Jesus' presence; we are still awaiting a more definitive (more concrete, more corporal) representation of the Son. We are awaiting the coming of the Lamb who seems to have been slain.

I want to interrupt the action (pause the movie?) for a moment to point out a few things.

The images of the Trinity are the One on the throne (the Father), the seven spirits (the Holy Spirit), and the Lamb (the Son). Interestingly, God's worshipers are introduced in the midst of the description of the Trinitarian God. It goes something like this: Father, twenty-four elders, Holy Spirit, four creatures, twenty-four elders, Son. God and those who worship him are all sort of mingled together. God created us in order to invite us into the very life of the Trinity.

In one of the few but precious meetings I had with Monsignor Luigi Giussani, founder of the lay Catholic movement Communion and Liberation, he spoke about the love of parent and child and husband and wife. He told me that these relationships are so important because they are echoes of "what is happening in God." He told me that in a Christian community we are called to be mothers and fathers to one another. John's description points to this mysterious intertwining of God and those who belong to him.

It is also worth noting that the Father and the Spirit are described well before the arrival of the Lamb. In fact, it seems that the Lamb is being awaited. Perhaps this is an image of the fact that Jesus was sent forth from the throne of his Father to come among us, and after his earthly ministry, he returned to the Father. Saint Paul repeats for us what was probably a well-known hymn at the time:

> Christ Jesus, who, though he was in the form of God, did not count equality with God a thing to be grasped, but emptied himself, taking the form of a servant, being born in the likeness of men. And being found in human form he humbled himself and became obedient unto death, even death on a cross. Therefore God has highly exalted him and bestowed on him the name which is above every name, that at the name of Jesus every knee should bow, in heaven and on earth and under the earth, and every tongue confess that Jesus Christ is Lord, to the glory of God the Father. (Philippians 2:5–11)

Paul would also write, "He who descended is he who also ascended far above all the heavens, that he might fill all things" (Ephesians 4:10). Jesus descended from the Father to us, and after his death and resurrection he again ascended to the Father.

I wonder if John is giving us an image of the Ascension, of this type of reunion of the Son with the Father and the Spirit. I say a "type" of reunion because Jesus himself said that the Father is always with him, yet he also said that he was returning to the Father (see John 17:13, 21–23). Thus we see how not only words but images falter before the mystery of God. Inadequate though these are, they are the tools we have to express the mystery of God. So let us return to the action!

The Sealed Scroll

John sees that the One seated on the throne is holding a scroll that is sealed with seven seals. Here we have the number seven again. If the scroll is sealed with seven seals, then it must be completely and perfectly sealed. It is held in the right hand of the Father and has writing on both sides. It must be the words of God or the plan of God—perhaps the blueprints of creation, complete with the explanations and reasons and meaning behind everything!

However, the scroll is completely sealed! It is wrapped in mystery. "And no one in heaven or on earth or under the earth was able to open the scroll or to look into it" (Revelation 5:3).

Who can explain the reason for his or her existence? Who can explain suffering? Sickness? Death? War? Famine? Evil? Why were you born when and where you were? Why did you wind up with those parents or fall in love with that spouse or live your life with those friends? Why are there tsunamis and hurricanes?

The scroll seems to be the image of all the questions of life, from small musings to the ultimate questions. John cries because no one is found worthy to open it; its mysteries are beyond our grasp. This cry is a beautifully human moment in the book of Revelation, because the ultimate questions of life and the melancholy before the fact that we can't answer them belong to the core of our humanity. The scroll is beyond our grasp, yet there it is before us!

A friend who directs plays once told me that if a gun is shown at any moment in a play, then it must be used at some point before the play ends; the audience expects it. Likewise, God the Father cannot wave a sealed scroll around and not expect us to want to see it! And not just to see it but to examine it, to look into it, to discover the meaning of all that is written within!

God holds the scroll before John in order to awaken his curiosity and desire. God has placed within us this desire to know the reason for everything; it is because of this curiosity and desire that reality itself leads us to seek God.

As a priest I have been in many hospital rooms and funeral homes, and I have seen the urgency of the human questions regarding suffering and death. I have faced my powerlessness and unworthiness to answer any of these questions. I have seen in my friends and parishioners the deep sadness of John, who cries before the sealed scroll, which no one is worthy to open.

These experiences and this moment in Revelation are manifestations of what Monsignor Luigi Giussani called the "religious sense."[1] Every human being has these questions, and these questions all come to a point at which they cannot be answered; they lead to the mystery we call God. To unseal the scroll is clearly impossible for us. Our only hope is that someone will come who can unseal it for us, that someone will come and reveal to us the mystery behind all of reality.

Plato expressed this four centuries before Christ:

[H]ow very hard or almost impossible is the attainment of any certainty about questions such as these in the present life. And yet I should deem him a coward who did not prove what is said about them to the uttermost, or whose heart failed him before he had examined them on every side. For he should persevere until he has attained one of two things: either he should discover or learn the truth about them; or, if this is impossible, I would have him take the best and most irrefragable of human notions, and let this be the raft upon which he sails though life—not without risk, as I admit, *if he can not find some word of God which will more surely and safely carry him.*[2]

One of the elders tells John, and all of us who await that *someone*, "Weep not; … the Lion of the tribe of Judah, the Root of David, has conquered, so that he can open the scroll and its seven seals" (Revelation 5:5).

The Lamb

And here he is! If Jesus always cedes supremacy to the Father, then why is the Lamb's arrival at this point so climactic? Because without Jesus the Father remains an inaccessible mystery. Jesus is our way to the Father, and no one can come to the Father except through him (see John 14:6).

The most important thing about God's Word is not its words but the truth that the words contain. However, without the words we can never know the truth. In Jesus the Word became flesh! He always points us to the Father, who is our ultimate destiny; and without the Son, the Word made flesh, we cannot know the Father.

The image of the Lamb, who looks "as though it has been slain," hearkens back to the unblemished lamb of Exodus, whose blood saved the firstborn of the Hebrew families from death. Jesus is the Lamb of God who saves us from death. That the Lamb *seems* like it was slain is a reference to the resurrection of Jesus. In our experience, when something is slain it stays dead. For Jesus, death is not final.

Perhaps even more interesting than the Old Testament imagery is the description of where the Lamb is standing: in the very midst of the throne (see also 7:17). How can this be? Isn't God the Father seated there? How can the Lamb be standing in the midst of the throne at the same time that God the Father is seated there?

While this is difficult to imagine—that is, to depict with an image—it is expressed very clearly with the words of the Creed. Jesus is "one in being with the Father." The oneness between the Father and the Son is also seen when the four living creatures and the twenty-four elders fall down in worship before the Lamb (5:8) in the same way they fell down in worship before the Father (4:9–10).

Think of the letters to the churches in which the major corrections had to do with their conceiving of themselves without Jesus. Think of Jesus, who reminds us that we can do nothing without him. Well, here we see that Jesus himself does not ever conceive of himself as alone, for he is one in being with the Father. He always lives in unimaginable unity and oneness with the Father.

The unity of Jesus with the Holy Spirit is also expressed with the seven horns and seven eyes that the Lamb has, which we are told are the seven spirits of God. The Lamb is never without his eyes, and Jesus is never without the Holy Spirit.

Presumably the seven spirits of God are still before the throne as well. These would be the Holy Spirit, who "proceeds from the Father and the Son." As the elders burn incense and sing hymns to the One on the throne and to the Lamb with the seven eyes, we can say of the Holy Spirit that "with the Father and the Son he is worshiped and glorified."

Let us now turn our gaze from the unity of the Trinity and toward the worshipers.

Those Around the Throne

Jesus is not only in the midst of the throne and the four creatures (who were themselves already around the throne, according to 4:6); he is also in the midst of the twenty-four elders. Thus Jesus is present with the Father and also present among his people; in him the unimaginable union between God and fallen humanity is made possible.

This hearkens back to the earlier image of Jesus standing in the midst of the seven lampstands or churches and all the implications of that image. Jesus is really present among us! He does not look down upon us from a distant heaven. He is present in heaven, but he is also in the midst of us. He has mixed himself up with us.

There is a beautiful scene in Krzysztof Kieslowski's *Decalogue One*, in which a young boy in communist Poland is incredulous before the fact that his aunt believes in God. The boy asks his aunt where God is. She embraces the boy, whereupon he tells her that he loves her. She then explains, "That's where God is."

God is in the midst of that love, in the midst of that human relationship. No theological or theoretical argument can witness to Christ as powerfully as the experience of Christ's presence in the midst of his people.

At Pentecost the apostles were not waiting for an apologetics class; they were waiting for the Holy Spirit to make Christ truly present among them. Merely talking about Jesus would be no good. It was his very presence that changed everything for those twelve men, and his presence would be recognized through the change it effected.

When Peter and John were arrested for preaching and healing in the name of Jesus, they were brought before the priests and elders who, "when they saw the boldness of Peter and John, and perceived that they were uneducated, common men, … wondered; and they recognized that they had been with Jesus" (Acts 4:13). The religious powers had only seen the inexplicable confidence of Peter and John in one other person: Jesus of Nazareth. Here they were seeing this same authority in two lowly fishermen!

Where did two lowly fishermen get such authority? Clearly it did not come from themselves. This is why their persecutors were in wonder before them, because their personal stature did not account for the authority they had.

It was not merely a matter of what Peter and John said but of who they were. And who were they? Men who had Christ living in them. These were the same apostles who had been afraid of the religious leaders, but now the resurrected life of Jesus had changed them.

This phenomenon is explained by the image of the twenty-four elders throwing down their crowns before the throne (see Revelation 4:10). This gesture, as well as that of falling down before the Lamb (Revelation 5:8), are acknowledgments that all of their authority is rooted in the Father, the Son, and the Holy Spirit.

The crowns on the elders indicate our reverence and respect for the saints and for Christians of our own time who have become authorities for us. Peter and John inspired wonder in their persecutors, but this wonder then led the persecutors to think of Jesus. I don't know the authority of Christ directly but through the witness of one who bears that authority now.

The writings and witnesses of saints like Paul, Augustine, Francis of Assisi, Teresa of Avila, Ignatius, and Thérèse of Lisieux hold great authority for us. Authority rests upon these particular men and women as the crowns rest on the heads of the elders; but the writings and witnesses of these men and women all point us to God, as represented by the elders throwing their crowns before his throne.

Members of religious orders and lay movements look upon their founders as fathers and mothers to them, for in the person of their founder they have received a certainty about Christ and a sure path to follow. The crown of Christ's authority adorns the heads of men and women throughout history, so that Christ can reach all men and women. My love for Christ does not exist abstractly but passes through the flesh of a people, particularly through those who have led and continue to lead me to him.

I have no problem when a Franciscan speaks with great reverence about Francis or a Focolare member speaks with great affection about Chiara Lubich; and I hope no one would fault me for speaking about Luigi Giussani with filial love. Christ mixes himself up with—that is, places his crown upon—particular people who make him palpably present to us, and these people lead our wondrous gaze to the One who makes them who they are. That is, they throw their crowns toward Christ.

Cardinal Roger Mahony shared a beautiful reflection on his time with Pope Benedict XVI during the pope's pastoral visit to the United States:

> The gentle and quiet manner of Pope Benedict touched me in the most vulnerable depths of my soul. I felt uplifted by our Shepherd and my heavy burdens somehow seemed lighter. How

did our Holy Father accomplish this? Through his consistent call to faithful discipleship in Jesus Christ, and his reassurance that we are truly saved by hope in our loving God![3]

Seeds of the Creed

So what have we seen in John's vision of heaven? We have seen the Father sitting on the throne (4:2–3). We have seen the Son in the midst of the throne and in the midst of the elders (5:6). We have seen the Holy Spirit with the Father in the form of seven torches burning before his throne (4:5) and with the Son in the form of the Lamb's seven horns and seven eyes, which are the seven spirits of God sent forth into the world (5:6). And we have seen the Church, represented by the twenty-four elders who are worshiping around the throne and also by the prayers of the holy ones, which are rising out of the censers that the elders hold in their hands (5:8).

This follows the pattern of Father, Son, Holy Spirit, Church that we find in the Church's creedal statements and sacramental formulas. In the Creed we profess belief in the *Father* Almighty, the only begotten *Son,* the *Holy Spirit* who proceeds from the Father and the Son, and the one, holy, catholic, and apostolic *Church.* The same pattern is clearly followed in the prayer of absolution for confession: "God, the *Father* of mercies, through the death and resurrection of his *Son,* has sent the *Holy Spirit* among us for the forgiveness of sins. Through the ministry of the *Church,* may God grant you pardon and peace...."

The Father is made known to us through the Son, and the Son sends us the Spirit to make himself present among us. When the Son becomes present among us, his mystical body

27

lives and grows in the world. This mystical body is the Church.

The vision of heaven given in Revelation shows the relationship of Father, Son, and Holy Spirit to be very dynamic. The Son is with the Father and also with his people. The Spirit burns before the throne of the Father, and he is at the same time sent into the world. The Church participates in this dynamic relationship: The followers of Jesus pray to the Father and the Son, at the same time the Spirit is sent to them, and they bear within and among them the very presence of the Son.

John shows us a fluid relationship between heaven and earth, a close communion between present history and eternal destiny. This indissoluble union is seen throughout the book of Revelation.

CHAPTER THREE

•

•

•

•

•

The Seven Seals: Jesus Is Present in the Mess of History
Revelation 6—7

We have already noted that the scroll sealed with seven seals seems to be God's plan. The fact that the Lamb is opening the scroll indicates that God's plan is fully revealed only through the Risen Christ—that is, the meaning of history is revealed in Jesus. This is important because knowing that things happen is different from knowing the meaning behind what is happening.

The apostles who ran away from Jesus during his passion saw many of the same events unfolding as did John, who followed Jesus all the way to Calvary. But if you read John's account of the passion, it seems that he understood much more than what he saw with his eyes. He recognized an authority in Jesus that was not crushed by suffering, humiliation, or death. In the midst of what seemed to be senseless violence, John was able to see the relentless presence of God's love.

Perhaps John was blind to this recognition when the events were unfolding, and it was Jesus' resurrection that made him look back and recognize the sacred and salvific meaning. The Church's liturgy affords John's incisive account of the passion the distinction of being read every Good Friday.

Without the Risen Christ all of our attempts to make sense of history and of our own lives will fall short. Marxism, for instance, sees class struggle as the key to history. While one's economic class can be hugely influential, it does not completely define the mystery of the human person, and so Marxism shows itself to be inadequate. Fascism does not recognize the inherent value of every human person by virtue of being created in God's image, and so it easily leads to cruel violence. Capitalism and individualism can place undue emphasis on human productivity and profitability and leave us with a skewed view of ourselves and the source of our value. Materialism does not take into account the fullness of the person, and it can lead to hopelessness.

The meaning of human life and history is beyond human ability to grasp, but Jesus can reveal it to us. For in his Gospel John proclaims that the logos became flesh—that is, the "meaning" became flesh! Thus it is only the Risen Christ, the Lamb who seems to have been slain, who is worthy "to take the scroll and to open its seals" (5:9). Only through his gaze can we glimpse the meaning of history.

The First Seal: Jesus Is the Alpha Who Will Also Be the Omega
When the first seal is opened, a rider on a white horse emerges, and he is given a crown as he goes out "conquering and to conquer" (6:2). When you look at this image in the context of the entire book of Revelation and of the New Testament, it seems clearly to be another portrayal of the Risen Christ. Some scholars dispute this. But in the final events, after the opening of the seventh and last seal, we will again see a man on a white horse, and he is called the Word of

God (see 19:11–13), which is what John calls Jesus in the prologue of his Gospel.

In Revelation Jesus refers to himself as "the Alpha and the Omega, the first and the last, the beginning and the end" (22:13). The man on the white horse is the beginning and the end of the revelatory seals: He comes at the opening of the first seal, and he is there again at the climactic culmination of the last seal.

The mystery here is that we have two simultaneous images of Jesus. He is both the Lamb who seems to have been slain and who is opening the seals, and he is the man on the horse who emerges at the breaking of the first seal. Knowing that even imagery falters before the mystery of God, let us try to glimpse the truths contained in these two images.

Let us recall that John's vision already revealed that Jesus is both in the midst of the Father's throne and in the midst of the elders: He is united to the Father in heaven at the same time that he is in the midst of the churches. In fact, if we look all the way back to the two creation stories that begin Genesis, we see that in the first story God is beyond creation, commanding existence into being, and in the second he is within creation, walking in the Garden of Eden. Something similar is happening here.

The Risen Christ—that is, the Lamb who seems to have been slain—is beyond his creation. At his resurrection Jesus broke beyond the limits the world imposes, and so his victory transcends time and space. Yet although Jesus' resurrection is once and for all, this victory must reach us in our own particular moment in history.

And here we come to Christ on the white horse, riding into history in order to conquer. But didn't he conquer already? Yes, the victory of the resurrection happened on that first Easter, but that victory happened again at the conversion of Paul, and later in history Christ conquered the heart of Augustine, and much later I saw his victory in men and women I have accompanied through the RCIA, as well as in my own life, where his victory over me is not once and for all but unfolds through time. In his mercy Jesus brings his resurrected victory into time, conquering and reconquering our fickle and wayward hearts.

In his first encyclical, *Redemptor Hominis*, John Paul II said that Jesus is the "center of the universe and history … [who] entered the history of humanity and, as a man, became an actor in that history."[1] Through his resurrected presence in the men and women who make up the Church, Christ united with the Father in heaven (the Lamb) remains an actor within history (the man on the white horse).

The Next Three Horses: War, Famine, and Death

After Jesus we get three horses and riders who are much less pleasant. The red horse is given power to take peace away from the world, so he is an image of war. When the black horse emerges, we hear about food being rationed at frighteningly high prices; he is an image of famine. For the rider of the pale green horse there is no poetic imagery. He is simply death, whether by war, famine, disease, or animal attack (see 6:3–8).

Who invited this tragic trio? The opening had such promise, and now these three come along! What kind of scroll is this?

Isn't God supposed to be nice? This kind of thing is exactly why people don't like the book of Revelation!

We are tempted to edit out this threesome, the way Disney whitewashes fairy tales it makes into movies. (Cinderella's sisters don't saw off their toes to fit the slipper, and we are not told that the mute mermaid never did get to marry the prince!) Unfortunately, deletion is not an option, for we are told at the end of this book, "If any one takes away from the words of the book of this prophecy, God will take away his share in the tree of life" (22:19). It also says that "if anyone adds to them, God will add to him the plagues described in this book" (22:18). So you can't even soften the blow by editing in some comic relief or perhaps some advice on how one might avoid meeting these heinous horsemen. They are real, and they are here, and you can't get rid of them!

In fact, you can't even say that these bad horsemen will only bring suffering upon bad people, because when the fifth seal is opened, we see the souls of martyrs, and we are told that there will be even more of them in the future. The opening of the sixth seal brings the worst possible natural disaster, and it will affect everyone. (Revelation 6:15 mentions seven different kinds of people who are affected by it, and remember that seven means complete.) Even Jesus' faithful followers are not spared.

There you have it: God's plan involves suffering, lots of it. You can complain that this book is fantastical and over the top, but think: Do you know anyone who has been spared suffering?

Often nonbelievers use human tragedy as their weapon against the Christian claim that God is loving. Non-Christians might refuse to believe that Christ is the Messiah because he did not take suffering away. But this final book of the Christian Scriptures is quite candid about the presence of suffering and quite audacious in its proposal that suffering is not merely present but is part of God's plan. It is coming out of his scroll!

The core of the Christian claim, however, is not that God is nice or loving, according to our current personal or cultural ideas of those words, but that God is with us. The opening of the seals tells us that the Risen Christ is with us in the world; he enters into every circumstance of our life. The Word became flesh and dwells among us! There is no time, place, or situation in which he is not.

The Risen Christ on his white horse comes forth into the world, in which war, famine, and death are also present. As he didn't remove the suffering of Roman occupation from the Jews, he does not remove suffering from us. In fact, if you look back at the letters, he tells Smyrna, "Do not fear what you are about to suffer" (2:10). He does not keep suffering from those he loves.

A Look at Suffering and God

It is beyond me to explain the meaning and reasons behind any particular instance of suffering. As a priest I have been asked to do it many times. I have followed the advice of a wise professor in the seminary, who warned us against ever giving in to the temptation to explain, as if we could know the mysterious depths of God. As an "other Christ," the best a priest can do, and the best any friend can do, is to be with those who suffer.

But here I want to take an honest look at human experience in order to glimpse the mystery of the coexistence of the merciful design of God and the reality of human suffering—that is, the white horse running alongside, or rather before, the red, the black, and the pale green.

First, let us take note of the fact that motherly and fatherly love does not require that the parent preserve the child from all possible suffering. (In fact, when parents attempt to do this, they risk rearing a spoiled child.) Mothers stand by and watch as their babies are given injections for vaccinations. If we could inhabit a baby's mind, I think we would find horrified confusion as he sees his mother allowing a relative stranger to put a needle in him. The mother allows it for his good, much as she allows the suffering entailed in the ingestion of vegetables.

As the child gets older, the parents may allow him or her to make mistakes that will likely lead to suffering. They may sometimes choose not to help the child financially, even if they are able, in order that the child may learn something about life.

We are children of God; God is our Father. A father can love his children and allow them to suffer. In his letter to the Laodiceans, Jesus says, "Those whom I love, I reprove and chasten" (Revelation 3:19). These words can be difficult to grasp initially, but they become more comprehensible when we look at real human experience. That God allows those other horsemen to exist is not a reason to doubt his love.

Second, if you consider suffering in your own life, can you recognize moments that were so painful that you would not want to live through them again, but that you would not delete from your life because they have made you who you are? There is a way in which suffering increases our humanity.

I saw this in New York in the days immediately following 9/11. I saw this in one of my students who lost his mother when he was quite young; it was clear that there was a depth to this boy that was not typical of his age. I saw it in a boy whose father died while he was in high school; we had a conversation at the wake that I don't think he would have been capable of before this tragedy.

Does this mean that it was good that 9/11 happened? Was it good that a mother or father of a young boy should pass away? No, these are bad things, and I cannot give a satisfactory explanation of the reasons for any one of them. But just as much as I cannot deny the presence of those three horsemen in Revelation or of bad things that happen in life, I cannot deny that I saw good flower from the midst of these bad things. The good is not any less real than the evil.

What is so horrifying in the horror movie *Invasion of the Body Snatchers*? The premise is that aliens take away people's emotions. Wouldn't that take away much suffering? Why are we horrified? I think it has something to do with the sense that to take away suffering is to take away something that makes us human. Another movie, *Eternal Sunshine of the Spotless Mind*, is about deleting painful memories, and there is something creepy about it.

What made Tom Brokaw's "greatest generation" so great? Apparently it was the Great Depression and World War II. These were two really, really bad things, and Brokaw recognizes that they led to greatness. And so, it seems, did the many people who made his book a best-seller.[2]

It can be easy to challenge whether God is present in the face of evil, and perhaps easier still to doubt his love as a result. However, let's look again at experience and ask the question, "Is it possible that evil has the last word, that evil has the final triumph?" This is an interesting question to ask. If we look at experience rather than theoretical argument, I think the answer from the human heart is a resounding and insistent no!

The Last Word

When the attack of 9/11 happened, the whole nation offered New Yorkers money, prayer, and even blood. When violence happens in schools, like the tragedies of Columbine and Virginia Tech, grief counselors help survivors deal with their loss. When someone suffers the loss of a loved one, there are usually friends and family who want to help the person engage once again in life.

Why? Why not just tell the survivors of 9/11 to give up and accept the fact that life stinks? Why not allow students who have experienced murderous violence to surrender to fear, depression, or neuroses? Why not let a surviving spouse, parent, or fellow student give up on life?

We all have a sense that this would be disgustingly inhuman and cruel. We share the conviction that evil does not and cannot have the last word, even if our efforts to combat it seem to make little difference.

Not only does evil not have the last word, but God's mercy can mysteriously use it for the good. The paradigmatic example of this is the passion and death of Jesus. The Church calls the sin of Adam a *felix culpa* or "happy fault": It was bad, but God made it good by sending a Savior; and the good of Jesus is way better than the bad of Adam.

Surely in your own life you can recognize moments when good came out of evil. My wonderful aunt wouldn't exist if my father's mother had not died the day after he was born and my grandfather had not remarried. For that matter, I might not exist, because my grandfather probably wouldn't have moved to the Bronx, where my father subsequently met my mother.

Tolkien offers a beautiful image of God's bringing good from evil in a creation tale he offers in *The Silmarillion*. The God figure is directing a harmonious choir, and an evil choir member decides he wants a solo part, so he sings out of tune. God then conducts a new harmony that utilizes this previously dissonant note. Each time the evil creature sings off key, God's harmonious inclusion of the note makes the music even more beautiful.

Tolkien expresses here the fact that no amount of evil can compromise God's infinite goodness. And God's glory is particularly resplendent when it raises good from the seemingly hopeless ashes of evil.

This is why there is no ultimate contradiction between God's loving design and the presence of evil within the unfolding of that design. The evils of the later horsemen do not need to be denied or tempered, because the victory of the Risen Christ is already present.

To go back to *The Little Mermaid*, Disney tampered with the story by tempering her suffering. There is no mention of the fact that every time she stepped on the ground, it would feel like knives piercing her feet, nor that the mermaid accepted death for love of the prince, even after he decided to marry another woman. In taking away the suffering, the moviemakers also took away the depth of love the story reveals. Disney's mermaid gets to marry a handsome prince; Hans Christian Andersen's mermaid finds eternal life. By removing sacrifice and suffering, our culture reduces the greatness to which we are called.

Revelation and Reality

Isn't it interesting that John tells us not to add or take away anything from this overwhelming vision? How often do I reject God by refusing to accept reality as he gives it? How often do I doubt God's goodness because he does not work according to my measure of how life should be or how things should turn out?

How many of us really trust that God is present in circumstances that are painful? How many of us faithfully beg for him in moments that seem meaningless? Do we really begin from the hypothesis that the foundation of reality is Jesus Christ, that all of reality springs mysteriously from God, who is Love?

After suffering a long and painful sickness, Monsignor Luigi Giussani was heard to say on his deathbed, "Reality has never betrayed me."[3] Suffering did not decrease his certainty of the presence of Christ; the cross of illness and impending death did not take his gaze away from the One who has risen and who was present to him always.

In the short documentary film *Greater: Defeating AIDS*, a Ugandan woman named Vicki speaks about her situation. Shortly after her husband abandoned her, leaving her with their three children, she discovered that he had infected her with AIDS. She was near despair until she met Rose Busingye, a nurse of great faith who had founded Meeting Point

International to help women such as Vicki. Rose told her that she was greater than her illness. These words slowly penetrated Vicki's self-pity (like the sword coming from Jesus' mouth!), and she joined this community of women who share in her suffering and, more importantly, share in the new life only Christ can give.

Vicki was not cured of AIDS, but her life changed. Something deep within her was waiting for Rose, waiting for Christ. Something in her knew that her suffering was not what defined her. In front of Rose, who looked upon her with the gaze of Christ, her faith and hope flourished.

We can be overrun and pounded by the red, black, and pale green horsemen, and yet at its deepest level the human heart seems to know that there is Someone else. Believer and non-believer alike intuit the presence of the man on the white horse, whose goodness is more powerful than any evil, whose victory promises to win over every defeat. Saint Paul wrote, "I consider that the sufferings of this present time are not worth comparing with the glory that is to be revealed to us" (Romans 8:18). In Revelation John says the same thing, albeit with lots of special effects and a much more colorful cast of characters.

Jews and Gentiles

Following the disasters unleashed by the opening of the sixth seal, John has a vision of four angels protecting the earth from the four winds until another angel puts the seal of God upon the foreheads of his servants. This might be an image of baptism; it is certainly an image of belonging to God.

Who are the 144,000 recipients of this seal? They are the chosen people of God, the Jews. Twelve thousand from each tribe of Israel are marked. The number twelve is always a reminder to us of God's chosen people, and multiplying any number by a thousand is a way of expressing many. These people are so important to salvation history that John specifically names each of the twelve marked tribes.

Then John sees "a great multitude which no man could number, from every nation, from all tribes and peoples and tongues, standing before the throne and before the Lamb, clothed in white robes, with palm branches in their hands" (7:9). The first group John saw were the Jews, and this second group are gentiles, for they come "from every nation."

Jesus said that he came first for the Jews and then for the gentiles (see, for instance, Matthew 10:5–6 and Mark 7:24–30). Paul reiterates this in his letters (see, for instance, Romans 1:16). Mark's Gospel tells us that Jesus multiplied loaves and fishes first for the Jews (Mark 6:34–44) and later for the gentiles (Mark 8:1–10). Interestingly, after feeding the Jews there were twelve baskets left over, and after feeding the gentiles there were seven baskets left over. Recall that seven means fulfillment, so while Jesus' mission begins with the Jews, it comes to fulfillment only when all the world is offered redemption by the Messiah.

The Jewish psalms look forward to this fulfillment, and the Jewish prophets foretell it. Psalm 117, for example, begins with the exclamation, "Praise the LORD, all nations! Extol him, all peoples!" and Isaiah prophesies,

It shall come to pass in the latter days
    that the mountain of the house of the LORD
shall be established as the highest of the mountains,
    and shall be raised above the hills;
and all the nations shall flow to it...(Isaiah 2:2)

If you are not of Jewish descent, you need not feel like a second-class citizen; rather rejoice that God has really entered into human history. He revealed himself not in some other-worldly spiritual way, recognizable only to religious geniuses, but within time and space. He chose Abraham, and through Abraham his tribe, and as the tribe grew, the knowledge of God spread. As the tribes distinguished themselves and became curiosities to others, God became increasingly present in history through them. The persecutions of the Jews were rejections of God and the way he chose to enter history, and these were not merely spiritual rejections!

Jesus came first to the Jews because they were chosen by his Father, but they were also the only ones capable of understanding who Jesus claimed to be. They were the people who believed in one personal God. When Jesus called the one true God his Father and went on to make divine claims for himself through his words and actions, the Jews were able to understand the weight of his claims in a way that the polytheistic gentiles could not. The few gentiles who did approach Jesus in the Gospels likely had a sense of his import because of the response they saw among the Jews.

The Jews will always remain the chosen people of God, as evidenced by the importance given to them in John's vision. They were chosen not to exclude the rest of us but that through them we may come to know the one true God, who fully reveals himself in his Son.

In light of our consideration of suffering inspired by the horsemen, it is interesting to read that those dressed in white robes "are they who have come out of the great tribulation; they have washed their robes and made them white in the blood of the Lamb" (Revelation 7:14). They have come through suffering and have been saved through the suffering of Jesus, who is now in the midst of the Father's throne (see 7:17). "For as we share abundantly in Christ's sufferings, so through Christ we share abundantly in comfort too" (2 Corinthians 1:5).

When an elder gives reasons for the rejoicing of this white-clad band, he mentions shelter and the satisfaction of hunger and thirst, but his list of comforts begins and ends with the presence of God on the throne (see Revelation 7:15–17). And so the deepest human needs are not answered by any social or political ideology or "ism." The answer to the human heart is a person. Those in white robes rejoice before the Son and before the Father. They rejoice before the One who was always there in the midst of every suffering and every lack. They rejoice before "the Alpha and the Omega, ... who is and who was and who is to come" (1:8).

CHAPTER FOUR

•

•

•

•

•

The Old and the New: The Plagues, the Two Witnesses, the Ark of the Covenant, and the Woman
Revelation 8—12

When the seventh and last seal is opened, there is silence in heaven. For Christians silence is not merely the lack of sound: It is the response of awe before the mystery of God. I once took some students on a hiking trip, and they talked all along the trail until a panoramic view from a cliff stunned them into a wondrous silence. So often we lack this silence, which should fill our hearts with wonder and expectation before beauty, before prayer or Mass, or in anticipation of God's presence in any of the sacraments.

The silence at the opening of the last seal prepares for the beginning of the final fulfillment, the full manifestation of the one true God, who is the destiny of all history and all existence. Fulfillment is once again signified by the number seven: Seven angels are given seven trumpets in a kind of liturgy in which another angel at God's altar offers incense and the prayers of God's holy ones.

Plagues and Freedom

The angel throws fire from the altar down to the earth, and chapters eight and nine go on to describe plagues that come to the world at the sound of the first six trumpets. These plagues are reminiscent of the plagues in the book of Exodus, preceding the freeing of the Jews from slavery in Egypt. Those plagues were meant to influence Pharaoh to allow the Jews their freedom. These plagues seem designed to bring sinners to repent of their sins, that is, to ask for their own freedom from sin and from its deathly consequences. We ask for this freedom in the penitential rite at the beginning of every Mass.

The primary sin is that of idolatry (see Revelation 9:20), after which are mentioned murder, magic, fornication, and theft (Revelation 9:21). This is significant because in Exodus, as God is giving the Ten Commandments to Moses on the mountain, at the foot of that mountain Aaron and God's people are sinning against the very first commandment, which prohibits idolatry, by creating a golden calf to be their god.

In a sense idolatry is at the core of every sin. I prefer my own designs to the design of God; I view my own way of seeing or acting or reacting as better than his. I act as if I know reality better than the Author of reality, as if I know the needs of my heart better than my heart's creator. Grace pierces through this illusion.

In Exodus the plagues are a prelude to political and economic freedom; in Revelation the plagues are a prelude to ultimate and definitive freedom. The Church has long seen Exodus and the Passover as a foreshadowing of the paschal mystery, and Revelation describes the manifestation of the final victory of the paschal mystery.

Jesus did not come into the world to free the Jews politically or economically. He made this clear when he said, "Render to Caesar the things that are Caesar's, and to God the things that are God's" (Mark 12:17). Political and economic freedom is important, and life is certainly hard without it, but Jesus offers union with the Father, which is a total, profound, and lasting freedom.

When immigrants separate from their families for the sake of the political freedom we enjoy in America, there is a pain that American freedom cannot take away, a pain that can be healed only by reuniting with their families. The freedom that comes from belonging to your family is an image of the freedom of belonging to the Father through the Son. When this freedom is experienced, it cannot be destroyed by poverty or persecution. Saint Damien on an island of lepers and Blessed Teresa in Calcutta, Saint Maximilian Kolbe and Bessie and Corrie ten Boom in Nazi concentration camps, and Father Walter Ciszek and Aleksandr Solzhenitsyn in Communist prisons are among the countless men and women who have borne witness to this truth.

The Small Scroll

In Revelation 10 an angel gives John a small scroll. If the big scroll that the Father gave to the Son is God's all-encompassing design for history, then this scroll is perhaps that piece of the design that John is to live and to reveal. Only the Lamb can open up the scroll of all scrolls, but we who are members of his body have little scrolls that represent our parts in the plan, the particular ways in which we are invited to participate with Jesus in the salvation of the world. If you sneak ahead and look at Revelation 20:12, you will see that at the final judgment, scrolls will be opened as we all come before God's throne.

The fullness of revelation happens only in Jesus, the meaning who has become flesh, but each Christian offers a particular glimpse into that history more or less clearly in proportion to his attachment to Christ. Note that in Revelation 10:3–4, John is told *not* to write down what he hears from the seven thunders, which again might represent the unfolding of God's ultimate plan (seven indicating completion). For John is not called to reveal the entire plan; his role is to reveal the small scroll that has been given to him.

In *The Chronicles of Narnia*, one of C.S. Lewis's recurring themes is that each character has to be concerned with his or her own part of the story and need not worry about the parts that are given to the others. We see this also at the end of John's Gospel: Peter is walking with Jesus, sees John, and asks, "Lord, what about this man?" Jesus answers, "What is that to you? Follow me!" (John 21:21–22).

The angel tells John that the scroll will be sweet in his mouth but bitter in his stomach, and John in turn tells us, "I took the little scroll from the hand of the angel and ate it; it was sweet as honey in my mouth, but when I had eaten it my stomach was made bitter" (Revelation 10:10). Once again we see joy and suffering side by side. When John takes the scroll, this is his yes to God's vocation for him. But as with every vocational path, it involves suffering.

I was joyful on the day I was accepted to the seminary and on the day of my ordination, but going forward in my vocation certainly involved sacrifice and suffering. We see great joy on the faces of newlyweds before the altar, but we know and they know that their yes will include heartache. So why do we say yes? Because there is a certainty that the One to whom we say yes is trustworthy, that "in everything God works for good with those who love him, who are called according to his purpose" (Romans 8:28).

The Two Witnesses

After John eats the small scroll, he is told to measure the temple of God and the altar. He is then told that the outer court of the temple will be trampled by the nations for forty-two months and that, during this period of 1,260 days, two witnesses will prophesy (see Revelation 11:1–3).

It is significant that the period of time given is equal to three and a half years. The book of Daniel, an apocalyptic book of the Old Testament, refers to a persecution of the Jewish people that will last for three and a half "times" (see Daniel 7:25). The setting of the Daniel story is the exile in Babylon, but it was written later and seems to allegorize the persecution of the Jews by the Greek king Antiochus IV, who desecrated the temple, made Jewish practices illegal (his men burned scrolls of the Law), and put many Jews to death (see 1 Maccabees 1:41–63). The Feast of Hanukkah is the celebration of the rededication of the temple after the persecutions of Antiochus IV.

Revelation contains many images similar to those in Daniel, and so three and a half years may be a traditional time period to ascribe to the persecution of God's people. It is also half of seven, which may signify incompletion or evil.

In Jewish law at least two witnesses were needed to testify to a judicial fact. Jesus refers to this when he says to the Pharisees, "In your law it is written that the testimony of two men is true" (John 8:17). The two witnesses of Revelation evoke the personages of Moses and Elijah. We are told that they have the power to close up the sky, as Elijah did in 1 Kings 17:1, and to turn water into blood and bring plagues, as Moses did in Exodus 7—11 (see Revelation 11:6).

Moses and Elijah are both instrumental in preparing the way for Jesus. Recall that when they had come out of Egypt, Moses prophesied to the Israelites, "The LORD your God will raise up for you a prophet like me from among you, from your brethren—him you shall heed" (Deuteronomy 18:15). Both Peter and Stephen interpreted this as a prophecy of Jesus (see Acts 3:22 and 7:37), and Pope Benedict XVI begins his book *Jesus of Nazareth* with an explanation of Moses' prophecy.[1]

Elijah, in turn, was expected to come before the Day of the Lord: "Behold, I will send you Elijah the prophet before the great and terrible day of the LORD comes" (Malachi 4:5). In accordance with this prophecy, Jesus referred to John the Baptist as the new Elijah as he came down the mountain after the Transfiguration (see Matthew 17:9–13). The Church's liturgy teaches us that the vision of the Transfiguration was given to the apostles to prepare them for the passion of Jesus.[2] And who did the apostles see standing with Jesus at this preparatory moment? Moses and Elijah.

Moses and Elijah also represent the Law and the prophets. Moses gave God's law to the Israelites, and Elijah was a great prophet of Israel. Jesus proclaims himself to be the fulfillment of the Law and the prophets: "Do not think that I have come to abolish the law and the prophets; I have come not to abolish them but to fulfill them" (Matthew 5:17); "Everything written about me in the law of Moses and the prophets and the psalms must be fulfilled" (Luke 24:44).

These two witnesses, then, are preparing the way for Christ as did Moses and Elijah, the Law and the prophets. Theirs is the last major scenario before the seventh trumpet heralds a vision that will evoke the incarnation, ministry, death, and resurrection of Jesus.

As John the Baptist foreshadowed Jesus not only with words but by suffering a violent death at the hands of Herod, so these two witnesses are killed by a beast that may be seen as an image of unjust temporal power that persecutes God's people. Their dead bodies are left "in the street of the great city which is allegorically called Sodom and Egypt, where their Lord was crucified" (Revelation 11:8). Jesus lamented over the real city of his crucifixion, "O Jerusalem, Jerusalem, killing the prophets and stoning those who are sent to you!" (Luke 13:34). Before Stephen, the first martyr, was stoned to death, he preached a similar theme: "Which of the prophets did not your fathers persecute? And they killed those who announced beforehand the coming of the Righteous One, whom you have now betrayed and murdered, you who received the law as delivered by angels and did not keep it" (Acts 7:52–53).

Every one of God's faithful is a kind of prophet, whether Jews whose persecution foreshadowed the saving death of Jesus or Christians whose lives herald that he has come into the world. In their deaths these two witnesses can represent all those who were killed for witnessing to the Lord: the Jews killed by Antiochus IV, the prophets, John the Baptist, Stephen, Peter, Paul, and all of the martyrs we saw under the altar of God at the opening of the fifth seal.

However, the two witnesses give one final testimony: That suffering and death will not have the last word. The breath of life is given back to them, and just as a voice from heaven was heard at the Transfiguration, a voice from heaven calls to the two witnesses, "saying to them 'Come up here!' And in the sight of their foes they went up to heaven in a cloud" (Revelation 11:12). There is a Jewish tradition that Moses was assumed into heaven, which the Letter of Jude seems to acknowledge when it speaks of the archangel Michael disputing with the devil over Moses' body (see Jude 1:9). And the second book of Kings tells of Elijah's ascension to heaven (2 Kings 2:11).

After the death and raising of the two witnesses, and then an earthquake, the survivors "were terrified and gave glory to the God of heaven" (Revelation 11:13). Interestingly, Antiochus IV was "astounded and badly shaken" when he discovered that the Israelites had risen against his armies and restored the temple (1 Maccabees 6:8). Recall that the scenario of the two witnesses began with the outer court of the temple being trampled by the nations, and when the scene concludes it has not yet been restored. This loose end will be taken care of at the sounding of the seventh trumpet.

The Seventh Trumpet: The Temple and the Ark
At the sounding of the seventh trumpet, "God's temple in heaven was opened, and the ark of his covenant was seen within his temple" (Revelation 11:19). Just as the political and

economic freedoms that man can achieve are not enough, so a temple that men can construct and restore is not enough. The temple building restored by the Israelites is a sign of a much greater fulfillment. In fact, the Lord told David (through the prophet Nathan) that he was not capable of building a house for God (see 2 Samuel 7:2–16).

Jesus indicated the inadequacy of the man-made temple when he said, "Do you see these great buildings? There will not be left here one stone upon another, that will not be thrown down" (Mark 13:2). More provocative than this was his prophecy, "Destroy this temple, and in three days I will raise it up" (John 2:19).

The true restoration of the temple cannot be effected by human hands but only by God. John is no longer concerned for the temple trampled by the nations, for God has now revealed his temple in heaven, which cannot be destroyed by any earthly power. In order to understand the nature of this temple, let us consider the ark of the covenant that is seen within it.

When this ark appears, what does it appear as? That is, what does John see? Let us read the passage, keeping in mind that chapters and verses were not part of the original text of Revelation or of any of the books of the Bible:

> Then God's temple in heaven was opened, and the ark of his covenant was seen within his temple; and there were flashes of lightning, loud noises, peals of thunder, an earthquake, and heavy hail.
>
> And a great sign appeared in heaven, a woman clothed with the sun, with the moon under her feet, and on her head a crown

of twelve stars; she was with child and she cried out in her
pangs of birth, in anguish for delivery. (Revelation 11:19—12:2)

The ark of the covenant is seen as a woman with child. The
original ark of the covenant held the tablets of the Law, given
to Moses by God (see Deuteronomy 10:5). We have already
seen that Jesus is the fulfillment of the Law, and so the child
held in the ark/woman is Jesus. He is described as "a male
child, one who is to rule all the nations with a rod of iron, ...
caught up to God and to his throne" (Revelation 12:5). Jesus
himself is the new covenant. He is the temple that is forever
restored through his resurrection, just as he promised.

As the Church is not merely an association but the bearer of
the presence of Jesus (as we saw with the lampstands and the
letters), so the covenant is not merely an agreement, as in the
old covenant, but a person, Jesus Christ. God's people do not
belong to an edifice but to a person; the Church is not a building but the mystical body of Christ. This image will be taken
up again when Revelation describes the New Jerusalem: "I
saw no temple in the city, for its temple is the Lord God the
Almighty and the Lamb" (21:22).

God is our freedom, God is our shelter, God is our temple.
Every temple and church building is but a sign that pales
before him whom it signifies. (And let's admit that some of
those signs are much paler than others.)

The Woman, the Son, and the Dragon

And a great sign appeared in heaven, a woman clothed with the
sun, with the moon under her feet, and on her head a crown of
twelve stars; she was with child and she cried out in her pangs
of birth, in anguish for delivery. And another sign appeared in
heaven; behold, a great red dragon, with seven heads and ten

horns, and seven diadems upon his heads. His tail swept down a third of the stars of heaven, and cast them to the earth. And the dragon stood before the woman who was about to bear a child, that he might devour her child when she brought it forth; she brought forth a male child, one who is to rule all the nations with a rod of iron, but her child was caught up to God and to his throne, and the woman fled into the wilderness, where she has a place prepared by God, in which to be nourished for one thousand two hundred and sixty days...

...The dragon...pursued the woman who had borne the male child. But the woman was given the two wings of the great eagle that she might fly from the serpent into the wilderness, to the place where she is to be nourished for a time, and times, and half a time. The serpent poured water like a river out of his mouth after the woman, to sweep her away with the flood. But the earth came to the help of the woman, and the earth opened its mouth and swallowed the river which the dragon had poured from his mouth. Then the dragon was angry with the woman, and went off to make war on the rest of her offspring, on those who keep the commandments of God and bear testimony to Jesus. And he stood on the sand of the sea. (Revelation 12:1–6, 13–18)

The first thing we must acknowledge in this passage is its reference to what the Church calls the *protoevangelium*, or "first gospel," which appears in Genesis:

> I will put enmity between you and the woman,
>> and between your seed and her seed;
> he shall bruise your head,
>> and you shall bruise his heel. (Genesis 3:15)

God is talking to the serpent who successfully tempted Eve. Church tradition tells us that God's warning to the serpent is also his promise to Eve's descendants that he will send us Jesus, who will crush the power of the serpent. Revelation 12 depicts the long-predicted struggle between the woman who bears Jesus and the ancient serpent. John explicitly tells us that the dragon is the ancient serpent (12:9), but who is the woman?

Mary, the mother of Jesus, is the first person who comes to mind before an image of a woman giving birth to Jesus. Jesus himself draws this connection in two significant moments in the Gospel of John. The first is the wedding feast at Cana, where Mary tells Jesus that they have run out of wine, and Jesus replies, "O woman, what have you to do with me? My hour has not yet come" (John 2:4).

A son's referring to his mother as "woman" was as shocking then as it would be now. When I ask my students what would happen if they went home and asked their mothers, "Woman, what's for dinner?" I hear a litany of punitive measures to which they are sure they would fall victim. However, Jesus is not being disrespectful toward Mary; he is almost certainly making reference to the woman mentioned in the proto-evangelium of Genesis. As if to say, "Mother, if I perform my first miracle here, then my ministry will begin; my war against the powers of evil will commence. You will become more than my mother; you will assume the role of the woman whose offspring crushes the ancient serpent."

Jesus calls his mother "woman" again from the cross, when he indicates John and says to Mary, "Woman, behold your son!" (John 19:26). The cross is perhaps the climax of the

55

battle, when Jesus is at the very jaws of the dragon that he is about to defeat. At this moment prophesied by his Father at the beginnings of creation, Jesus proclaims Mary to be the woman and he her offspring who will crush the serpent.

With these moments in mind, let us ponder the fact that in the image the woman is giving birth to her son. Mary gave birth to Jesus at the beginning of his earthly life, and at the wedding feast at Cana she "gives birth" to his public ministry. For doesn't his ministry begin as a response to her simple request? And when she tells the waiters, "Do whatever he tells you," she is echoing the yes she gave to the original announcement of Jesus' coming.

Likewise, her standing at the foot of the cross is another yes to Jesus' saving action, which he could not have performed had she not given birth to him in the flesh. Jesus' battle with the devil began at his incarnation, which evil resisted through the cruelty of King Herod; it intensified with the beginning of his public ministry, which the devil tried to fight by tempting Jesus in the desert; it was completed at the cross, which seemed to be evil's finest hour but instead was Jesus' hour of glory. Perhaps all of these moments are expressed in the woman bearing her son before a dragon ready to devour him.

The woman escapes the power of the dragon, and in his fury he spews forth a river of water, but the earth swallows up the water, and it never touches the woman. Could this be a scriptural indication of the doctrine of the Immaculate Conception? A flood of water evokes the flood in Genesis, which came forth as a punishment for sin. This woman was not touched by the water. Is it because she has no sin?

The woman might also be an image of Israel. For Jesus came forth from the people of Israel, sometimes referred to in the Old Testament as "daughter Zion" or "daughter Jerusalem." As the woman cries out in the pangs of birth, Israel suffered greatly in her history.

A major way that God's chosen people witness to his presence in history is simply by being different from the peoples around them. The Israelites who were faithful to the Lord would never assimilate into neighboring or ruling cultures. Their belief in one God and their keeping of his laws and ordinances made them different, and the difference was not always welcome. They were slaves in Egypt, exiles in Babylon, and victims of the aforementioned Greek persecutions. In the time of Jesus they suffered the burden of Roman occupation and rule. That the Jews even existed at the time of Jesus and were thus present to understand his claim to be the one and only God was because of the faithful endurance of many Jews, from Abraham down to the remnant of Israel.

Lastly, the woman can be seen as an image of the Church. We have already noted that the presence of Jesus in the midst of the Church is a recurring theme in Revelation. The Church bears the presence of Christ in the world.

In chapter one of this book, we saw that the book of Revelation was written in the context of a Church that had already come through at least one period of persecution and was likely in the midst of another one. The Christians at that point knew that bearing Christ to the world entails suffering, and Revelation expresses this when it warns, "The dragon was angry with the woman, and went off to make war on the rest of her offspring, on those who keep the commandments of God and bear testimony to Jesus" (Revelation 12:17).

The Accuser

If you are an astute reader, you will have noticed that in my extensive quote of the woman/son/dragon passage above, I edited out a piece in the middle of it. If you recall also that Revelation warns us not to add or take away from the book, then you might be frightened for me, or you might be accusing me. Fear no more! Hold your accusations! We will now look at that passage in order to consider one of Revelation's most interesting descriptions of the devil.

> Now war arose in heaven, Michael and his angels fighting against the dragon; and the dragon and his angels fought, but they were defeated and there was no longer any place for them in heaven. And the great dragon was thrown down, that ancient serpent, who is called the Devil and Satan, the deceiver of the whole world—he was thrown down to the earth, and his angels were thrown down with him. And I heard a loud voice in heaven, saying, "Now the salvation and the power and the kingdom of our God and the authority of his Christ have come, for the accuser of our brethren has been thrown down, who accuses them day and night before our God." (Revelation 12:7–10)

In the book of Revelation, the devil is called "the accuser." We see this in the Old Testament as well. The prophet Zechariah had a vision of the high priest Joshua standing before the angel of the Lord, while Satan stood at his right hand to accuse him.

> Then he showed me Joshua the high priest standing before the angel of the LORD, and Satan standing at his right hand to accuse him. And the LORD said to Satan, "The LORD rebuke you, O Satan! The LORD who has chosen Jerusalem rebuke you! Is not this a brand plucked from the fire?" Now Joshua was standing before the angel, clothed with filthy garments. And the angel said to those who were standing before him, "Remove the filthy

garments from him." And to him he said, "Behold, I have taken your iniquity away from you, and I will clothe you with rich apparel." (Zechariah 3:1–4)

Notice the way God looks at the filthily clad Joshua and the way Satan looks at him. It seems that Satan sees Joshua as guilt-ridden and undeserving, while God sees him as a brand plucked from the fire, as someone he has chosen. Joshua belongs to God.

There is a beautiful scene in Sister Helen Prejean's *Dead Man Walking*. The mother of a man who has committed a horrendous crime says that it was good that the guards did not let her embrace her son on her last visit before his execution. Had they let her embrace him, she never would have let him go. She looks past everything he has done that has labeled him a criminal and sees the core of who he is, her son.

This mother is an icon of God's love for us. God looks past all Joshua's guilt and looks at his heart, and he sees the greatness of a man standing before his throne in all his filth and hoping for the merciful gaze of the Lord. Satan might have had many reasons why God's mercy for Joshua was undeserved, but mercy does not need to be deserved; it needs to be sincerely hoped for and desired.

In the Gospel of John, Jesus says, "Him who comes to me I will not cast out" (John 6:37). What is required is not that the guilty deserve the love of Jesus but that he desire it enough to *come* to Jesus. The purpose of our Christian life is not to rack up good deeds but to prepare our hearts to humbly come before God's throne, admitting our sin, showing our filth, and desiring the tender mercy of a loving Father. You can do countless good deeds, but if you do not recognize your undeservedness, and if your heart is not humble like the heart of a child, you will not approach Jesus and therefore will not receive his mercy.

C.S. Lewis's *The Great Divorce* is a wonderful fable that shows that a humble heart is essential for salvation. It tells of murderers who sought mercy inhabiting heaven, while more "respectable" types remain on the outskirts, clinging to their pride.

As we see in the above passage from Zechariah, a humble heart before God the Father vanquishes all of Satan's power. It doesn't matter how many, how true, or how heinous the accusations are; nothing can break the Father's embrace of a son or daughter who seeks him.

The Accused

Because we are fallen, we all carry a bit of Satan's mentality within us. How often do we look at ourselves with the merciless gaze of Satan toward Joshua? We completely forget God's mercy and look only at our measure of what we do or don't deserve. I can't save myself from Satan's power. I need someone, or rather Someone, outside of me.

It is not uncommon for people to stay away from confession for years because of sins that they consider to be particularly shameful. When I hear such a confession, my heart goes out to the penitent, who for too long thought that his or her sin was too great for God to forgive. I think to myself, if I can feel such tenderness for this penitent, how much more must the Father's tenderness be? I do all I can to assure this person of the Father's forgiveness.

However, when I commit a sin of which I am particularly ashamed, I cannot convince myself of God's love, no matter how hard I try. I need God's gaze to come to me through someone else. I need the Father to cast out the nagging and persistent accuser, who accuses night and day.

Our culture often connives with our accusing fallen nature. It amplifies the accuser by broadcasting accusations. Papers are sold and TV ratings are won by parading before us the latest sinner whom it is fashionable to hate or ridicule. How easy it is for those who do not know or love these people to associate them with their shameful deeds. Each newly notorious name might carry media sales on its coattails and offer false self-satisfaction to accusing gawkers.

A New York paper once boasted a photo of two teenagers who were suspected of a violent crime, with the headline "On a Mission of Hatred." Perhaps the accused were on a premeditated mission, or perhaps they acted rashly and irrationally. What "mission," however, was the paper on? Certainly that front page was planned by someone, probably an adult, whom you would assume would know and react more maturely than a teenager. Yet that page was certainly meant to incite disgust, and perhaps even hatred, toward the accused.

In a letter to the bishops in 2009, Pope Benedict wrote,

> At times one gets the impression that our society needs to have at least one group to which no tolerance may be shown; which one can easily attack and hate. And should someone dare to approach them, ... he too loses any right to tolerance; he too can be treated hatefully, without misgiving or restraint.[3]

I don't deny the horror of sin. But Christ died and rose, he fought and won the victory, so that sin and accusation would never have the last word. "Though your sins are like scarlet," Isaiah prophesied, "they shall be as white as snow" (Isaiah 1:18). I rejoice that mercy and redemption are possible for every repentant sinner who comes to Christ, because this means it is possible for me!

I am horrified by the thought that any person would be branded forever by sins—that is, defined by the accusations of the accuser rather than redeemed by the love of the Father. The casting out of the accuser makes it possible for our names to be cleared of every sin and accusation and written forever in the Book of Life (see Revelation 3:5).

Fulfillment and Resistance

The number seven signifies completion and fulfillment; so the sounding of the seventh trumpet brings with it a depiction of Jesus' incarnation, that is, his coming into the world in the flesh he has received from the woman. Any revelation of God will meet with resistance; since the Incarnation is the greatest revelation of God, it meets with the fiercest resistance.

The dragon resists the birth of the woman's son from the outset. He does not have victory over the son, because the son is snatched up to God's throne. After being thrown to earth, the dragon pursues the woman. When his flood of hatred cannot touch her, he decides to make war on her offspring.

Who are the woman's offspring? All of those who belong to the body of Christ. And this becomes clear when God's revelation and the devil's resistance are at their most intense: at the cross. While God is revealing his love through Jesus' sacrifice and the devil is resisting with violence, hatred, and death, Jesus tells Mary, "Woman, behold, your son," and he tells

John, "Behold, your mother" (John 19:26, 27).

The flesh of Jesus came from Mary, and Jesus remains truly present in all subsequent history through the flesh and blood members of his Church. She who is the mother of the body of Christ is also the mother of the mystical body of Christ. The "rest of her offspring" will discover in their turn that the presence of God in the world meets intense resistance. If they remain united with Jesus, they will discover that the resistance is as nothing before his presence.

Recall the scene in *The Passion of the Christ* when the devil figure and Mary are on opposite sides of the Via Dolorosa, looking one another in the eye. The staring match is broken by Mary, who looks at Jesus, thus showing us where victory lies. Recall Jesus' letters to the churches: The victor will be the one who remains with his eyes, his heart, and all of his love fixed upon Christ.

•

•

•

•

•

Devilish Imitations
Revelation 13

Revelation 12:9 tells us, "The great dragon was thrown down, that ancient serpent, who is called the Devil and Satan, the deceiver of the whole world," and the chapter concludes with his taking his battle position. And what position is the devil, the deceiver, going to take? He is going to try to take God's position. If God is not going to give all of his power and honor and glory to Satan, then Satan has no use for God.

In fact, even if God did give the devil all of his power, honor, and glory, the devil would not be satisfied. Rather he would be annoyed that it had to be given to him, that it didn't originate with him. The devil doesn't much like reality, because in reality God is God and the devil is a creature. The devil therefore is a deceiver who likes illusion and artifice, by which he can pretend to be God.

Since the devil hates the fact that God has not given him all power, honor, and glory, he also hates anyone who has been given any share in God's divine life. He hates the Son and the Holy Spirit because they are God. He hates Mary because she was invited to participate in a particular way in the Incarnation and because she was preserved from sin, that rejection of God upon which Satan feeds. He also hates the baptized, who have become members of the body of Christ and thus share in the divine life of God. And he hates all humans because we are made in God's image and thus share in God's glory by virtue of our very existence.

The devil wants to lead us away from God. But he is smart enough to know that every human heart was made for God and longs for God. Therefore the best way for him to fight against God is to look like him, so that he can lead hearts away from him.

A boy who wants to take advantage of a girl can't just go up to her and say, "Hey, have sex with me, and then leave me alone." He has to pretend to love her, because he knows that her heart is made for love and that she will respond to what looks like love. A con artist has to seem as if he has authority and has the best interests of his victims in mind; otherwise he will have no chance of conning them. He can't just come out and say, "Give me your money because I want it, and I couldn't care less about your financial stability." Our hearts are attracted to true friendship, and so the con man must make himself look like a knowledgeable friend.

The problem with the devil is that whenever he tries to look like God, the result is a strange and twisted distortion. Imagine a Miss America pageant in which a losing contestant will not accept the reality that she is not the winner. She accosts the new Miss America, rips off her sash, and steals her crown. Surely the photographers will take pictures of this woman, but she's not going to look at all like Miss America. She's going to look like a deranged woman with a ripped sash and a crooked crown.

Or imagine that at the end of the Super Bowl, the losing team can't accept the reality that they have actually lost. (Remember the 2008 Patriots?) What if they pull a surprise attack on the winners during the postgame celebration and, after a prolonged brawl, capture the trophy? Surely their pictures will make the papers, but they won't look at all like Super Bowl winners. They will look like a bruised and bloodied gang of criminals.

After the devil has been thrown down from heaven, he refuses to accept his defeat. He tries to make himself out to be the eternal winner, that is, God. As we saw in our first vision of heaven, God is a Trinity of persons, Father, Son, and Holy Spirit. Satan fights back with his own devilish version of the trinity: a dragon, a first beast, and a second beast. (I told you it would be a twisted distortion!)

The First Beast of the Devil's "Trinity"

And I saw a beast rising out of the sea, with ten horns and seven heads, with ten diadems upon its horns and a blasphemous name upon its heads. And the beast that I saw was like a leopard, its feet were like a bear's, and its mouth was like a lion's mouth. And to it the dragon gave his power and his throne and great authority. (Revelation 13:1–2)

The dragon gives his authority to the first beast; this is in imitation of the Father, who gives his authority to the Son. At the end of Matthew's Gospel, Jesus told the disciples, "All authority in heaven and on earth has been given to me" (Matthew 28:18). This fact is recognized by a voice from heaven at the very moment the devil is thrown down: "Now the salvation and the power and the kingdom of our God and the authority of his Christ have come" (Revelation 12:10).

One of the first things people noticed about Jesus was the authority with which he spoke (see Mark 1:22). And Jesus never used his authority to glorify himself but to give glory to the Father. We see this in the very beginning of Jesus' beautiful prayer to the Father in chapter seventeen of John's Gospel: "Father, the hour has come; glorify your Son that the Son may glorify you" (John 17:1).

That the beast is a mockery of Jesus is also clear when we read, "One of its heads seemed to have a mortal wound, but its mortal wound was healed" (Revelation 13:3). Recall the vision of Jesus in heaven as the Lamb who looked "as though it had been slain" (Revelation 5:6). Obviously this second person of the devilish trinity is a distortion that does not look like Jesus at all.

Revelation chapter seventeen will tell us that the seven heads of the beast represent seven kings, and the ten horns represent ten kings (verses 10, 12). Chapter seven of the Old Testament book of Daniel describes a very similar vision, except that there are four separate beasts: One looks like a lion, the other like a bear, the third like a leopard, and the last and most frightful has ten horns. Daniel's first three beasts each represent a king, and the fourth beast represents a kingdom from which there will be ten kings. The beast of Revelation seems to be a conglomeration of all these beasts and thus may represent every kingdom whose authority does not defer and refer to God the Father. This can be seen in the seven heads, the seven as always referring to completion and thus the seven heads to *every* ungodly earthly power.

The seven heads are also likely a reference to the traditional seven hills of Rome, thus making this beast, who wields the devil's authority, a symbol of the Roman Empire. To the early Christians the power of Rome must have seemed truly devilish. The empire had long oppressed God's chosen people, and with the advent of Christianity, it claimed for itself the "authority" to arrest and kill Christians, members of the very body of Christ.

The Roman Empire even had a tradition of ascribing divinity to its emperor. One of the ways that persecuted Christians would be "invited" to deny Christ was to participate in a gesture of sacrificial worship toward the emperor.

And there was no apparent escape from this evil empire, because it seemed to stretch everywhere. Those imperiled Christians would have understood John well when he wrote, "The whole earth followed the beast with wonder. Men worshiped the dragon, for he had given his authority to the beast, and they worshiped the beast, saying, 'Who is like the beast, and who can fight against it?'" (Revelation 13:3–4). For during times of persecution, the Roman Empire really was calling for worship, and its power must have seemed unconquerable by any human standards, whether military, political, or economic.

So the Christians for whom John is writing are suffering under an earthly power that is literally trying to take the position of God in their lives, not by love, as Jesus does, but by threat and force. This beast has the mark of the devil's distorted imitation. He is similar to Jesus because he has been given authority, but he doesn't look like Jesus at all, because his authority is one that does not love and give life but rather threatens with death. The beast's authority does not lead us to God the Father but tries to take his place.

A friend who teaches history explains to his students that even if he were an atheist, he would want to belong to a nation that recognizes itself to be "under God." That recognition is an admission that the state is not the ultimate authority and that my life defers to something greater.

The Number of the First Beast

John tells us that the evil reign of this first beast will be forty-two months. Recall that this seems to be a traditional time period ascribed to the persecution of God's people. The beast also has a number, 666, and we are told that the number stands for a person (Revelation 13:18).

A number might be ascribed to a person in the ancient world by taking number values assigned to letters, through a kind of numerology called *gematria*. When you add up the letters of a person's name, you have the person's number. Many have noted that "Caesar Nero" in Hebrew adds up to 666. It's quite possible that John is referring to Nero here as the symbol of every persecuting emperor. Recall what was said in the introduction about how we might use Hitler to refer to subsequent dictators. The problem is that Revelation seems to have been written originally in Greek. However, perhaps giving the Hebrew number value was John's way of making his reference that much more discreet.

Others note that 666 is the numerical value of the phrase "Caesar is God" according to the Greek. So perhaps John is saying that the beast is any emperor or any ruler who puts himself in the place of God.

The only place that the number 666 seems to appear in the Old Testament is in the first book of Kings. Six hundred sixty-six talents is the weight of gold that King Solomon received every year, making him renowned for his wealth (see 1 Kings 10:14). Later we learn that "King Solomon excelled all the kings of the earth in riches and in wisdom. And the whole earth sought the presence of Solomon to hear his wisdom, which God had put into his mind" (1 Kings 10:23–24).

Notice that the wisdom comes from God, while this passage does not say the same about the riches. Wisdom is the one and only thing that Solomon had asked from God, and God was thus pleased to bestow understanding upon Solomon. The riches were secondary (see 1 Kings 3:4–14).

Interestingly, this account of Solomon's wealth comes just before the book tells us of Solomon's sins, which involved turning to foreign wives and strange gods and doing evil in the sight of the Lord. Perhaps Solomon's downfall began by preferring his 666 talents of gold to the wisdom God had bestowed on him. He had forgotten his first love and relied on riches more than God's wisdom. When gifts of God are no longer recognized as coming from God and pointing us toward him, they begin to be seen as ends in themselves. They become idols, that is, distortions of their true nature and obstacles to God.

The numbers sixty and six do appear in the book of Daniel, which seems to have many echoes in the visions of Revelation. That book tells us that

> King Nebuchadnezzar made an image of gold, whose height was sixty cubits and its breadth six cubits. He…sent to assemble the satraps, the prefects, and the governors, the counselors, the treasurers, the justices, the magistrates, and all the officials of the provinces to come to the dedication of the image…. And

the herald proclaimed aloud, "You are commanded, O peoples, nations, and languages, that when you hear the sound of the horn, pipe, lyre, trigon, harp, bagpipe, and every kind of music, you are to fall down and worship the golden image that King Nebuchadnezzar has set up; and whoever does not fall down and worship shall immediately be cast into a burning fiery furnace." (Daniel 3:1–2, 4–6)

It was the refusal of Daniel and his two companions to worship this golden statue that landed them in the fiery furnace, from which they were saved by a mysterious man who looked like a "son of the gods" (Daniel 3:25). This golden statue, which demanded worship and threatened death to those who refused, was not dissimilar to the Roman emperors who were set up as gods.

Lastly, the number six could simply be seen as a sign of imperfection, falling just short of seven, which is the number of fulfillment. It is as if six is trying to be seven, as the devil is trying to be God. However, if six connotes imperfection, then perhaps a person whose identity adds up to 666 is simply "really, really, really" bad, as opposed to God, who is "holy, holy, holy" (Revelation 4:8).

The Second Beast of the Devil's "Trinity"

As the first beast attempts to imitate the Son, the second beast tries to look like the Holy Spirit. This second beast "exercises all the authority of the first beast" (Revelation 13:12).

In John's Gospel Jesus speaks of the Spirit's carrying on his authority:

When the Spirit of truth comes, he will guide you into all the truth; for he will not speak on his own authority, but whatever he hears he will speak, and he will declare to you the things that are to come. He will glorify me, for he will take what is mine and declare it to you. All that the Father has is mine; therefore I said that he will take what is mine and declare it to you. (John 16:13–15)

And so this sharing of authority is the similarity.

The distortion is seen when we read that the second beast also "makes the earth and its inhabitants worship the first beast" (Revelation 13:12). Again, there is not love or witness or invitation but rather force, just as Nebuchadnezzar tried to force the officials to worship a statue and the Roman Empire tried to force early Christians to worship the emperor.

The imitation continues as we see the second beast "making fire come down from heaven," as the Holy Spirit did at Pentecost. That this beast is part of the devil's trinity is evident when we read that he uses his signs in order to deceive the earth's dwellers.

By the signs which it is allowed to work in the presence of the beast, it deceives those who dwell on earth, bidding them make an image for the beast which was wounded by the sword and yet lived; and it was allowed to give breath to the image of the beast so that the image of the beast should even speak, and to cause those who would not worship the image of the beast to be slain. Also it causes all, both small and great, both rich and poor, both free and slave, to be marked on the right hand or the forehead, so that no one can buy or sell unless he has the mark, that is, the name of the beast or the number of its name. (Revelation 13:14–17)

The second beast breathes life into the image of the beast, just as the Holy Spirit is the life breath of the Church, the body of

Christ. In fact, *spirit* means "wind" or "breath," and a great wind heralded the coming of the Holy Spirit at Pentecost. By conjuring a second beast that makes the image of the first beast come alive, it seems that the devil is trying to make his imitation of the relation between the Spirit and the Son as accurate as possible.

For the Holy Spirit always makes Jesus, the perfect image of the Father, present in the world and in the Church. This happens for the first time at the Annunciation. Mary asks how she can be the mother of Jesus, because she is a virgin, and she is told, "The Holy Spirit will come upon you" (Luke 1:35). The Holy Spirit thus brings about the beginning of the human life of Jesus, the entrance into the world and in the flesh of the living image of the Father.

When the apostles are enlivened by the Spirit at Pentecost, they preach with the same certainty and authority as did Jesus. In them Jesus' image is made alive. Just so his image is made alive again when Peter is filled with the Holy Spirit before the Sanhedrin, preaches with certainty, and is recognized as a companion of Jesus (see Acts 4:5–13). The image of Jesus lives again in Stephen, who when he is filled with the Holy Spirit, forgives his persecutors, just as Jesus did. Stephen also commends his own spirit to Jesus, in the same way Jesus commended his spirit to the Father (see Luke 23:34, 46; Acts 7:54–60).

The Holy Spirit also makes Jesus alive for us in the Eucharist. In the Eucharistic Prayer the priest (acting *in persona Christi* by virtue of having received the Spirit at his ordination) asks the Father to send the Holy Spirit upon the bread and wine so that it can become Christ's body and blood. From the beginnings of the Church, the Holy Spirit has been making Jesus present and alive in all times and places where his followers live.

The devil seems to know this. And since the presence of Jesus in the world signals his defeat, and he will not accept the reality of that defeat, he tries to play God. In this case playing God means trying to look like the Holy Spirit and Jesus through the second and first beasts.

CHAPTER SIX

•

•

•

•

•

Love Versus Power

Revelation 13—16

Next we see the second beast stamping the image of the first beast on all people (see Revelation 13:16–17). This is another thing this tricky trinity is trying to copy from the Holy Trinity.

Recall that when the day of the Lord's wrath is described after the opening of the sixth seal, an angel places the seal of the living God on the foreheads of God's servants (see Revelation 7:1–3). This seal evokes the permanent sacramental seal of baptism, and John the Baptist prophesied that Jesus would baptize with the Holy Spirit (see Mark 1:8). The Holy Spirit makes us members of the body of Christ, that is, "other Christs." In imitation of this, the second beast seeks to stamp people with the image of the first beast.

Let us look at the great variety of people who will be forced to receive the mark of the beast: "both small and great, both rich and poor, both free and slave" (Revelation 13:16). This is clear evidence of the devil's jealousy of God, whose love freely attracts all kinds of people. For John has already told us of the heavenly vision, that of "a great multitude which no man could number, from every nation, from all tribes and peoples and tongues, standing before the throne and before the

Lamb" (Revelation 7:9). And in the Letter to the Galatians, Paul reminds us, "For as many of you as were baptized into Christ have put on Christ. There is neither Jew nor Greek, there is neither slave nor free, there is neither male nor female; for you are all one in Christ Jesus" (Galatians 3:27–28).

That early Christianity was spreading among all kinds of people is witnessed even by one of the persecutors. Pliny was a governor in Pontus-Bithynia from AD 111 to 113. He tried to carry out the policy of keeping Christianity in check, and he had some questions about the methods he should use in his investigations and interrogations. So he wrote a letter to the Emperor Trajan, excerpts of which give us a glimpse of the diversity of the early Christians and what they had to face:

> I have never participated in trials of Christians. I therefore do not know what offenses it is the practice to punish or investigate, and to what extent.
>
> ...
>
> [I]n the case of those who were denounced to me as Christians, I have observed the following procedure: I interrogated these as to whether they were Christians; those who confessed I interrogated a second and a third time, threatening them with punishment; those who persisted I ordered executed.... There were others possessed of the same folly; but because they were Roman citizens, I signed an order for them to be transferred to Rome.
>
> ...
>
> [T]he matter seemed to me to warrant consulting you, especially because of the number involved. For many persons of every age, every rank, and also of both sexes are and will be endangered. For the contagion of this superstition has spread not only to the cities but also to the villages and farms.[1]

Among the Christians were Romans and non-Romans, young and old, low rank and high rank, men and women, city dwellers and farmers. As annoying as this must have been to government officials, it was much more annoying to the devil. And the only way he could imitate this conversion of multitudes to the Trinitarian God was to force conversions to his deceptive images. Let us look at another excerpt from Pliny's letter:

> Those who denied that they were or had been Christians, when they invoked the gods in words dictated by me, offered prayer with incense and wine to your image, which I had ordered to be brought for this purpose together with statues of the gods, and moreover cursed Christ—none of which those who are really Christians, it is said, can be forced to do—these I thought should be discharged. Others named by the informer declared that they were Christians, but then denied it, asserting that they had been but had ceased to be, some three years before, others many years, some as much as twenty-five years. They all worshipped your image and the statues of the gods, and cursed Christ.[2]

It is interesting that the Roman governor was not satisfied if the accused merely denied Christ but required that they offer sacrifice to images of the emperor and to statues of the gods. It is as if he understood the words of Jesus, "He who is not with me is against me" (Matthew 12:30). There will be no room for neutrality in this battle. Love is either true or false.

The only way Satan knows to include all kinds of people in his army is through force. The second beast could have anyone who did not worship the image of the first beast put to death, just as Pliny threatened the accused Christians with punishment and death if they did not worship the image of the emperor.

The Force of Satan Versus the Love of God

We have seen the precision with which the devil tries to imitate God by the parallels between the dragon, the first beast, and the second beast on one hand and the Father, the Son, and the Holy Spirit on the other. Yet at the same time we see how horrifyingly he misses the mark. I think the fatal flaw can be seen in the difference between forced worship and free worship.

The devil imitates the dynamics of the Trinitarian God, but the very essence of God seems to escape him. Yes, the Father gives authority to the Son; yes, the Son is made present by the Spirit. But why? What is at the heart of this? Who is God at his/their very core?

The devil and, sadly, many people conceive of God as power—that is, they see power as the most essential attribute of God. This is simply not true, and I don't know if we should call it a devilish lie or a devilish misconception. In his first encyclical Benedict XVI reminds us that God is Love.[3]

God certainly has power, which we can see in creation and in his miracles. However, God can show himself without power, as he did by becoming an infant and ultimately by dying on the cross.

In fact, it seems that it is at the cross that Jesus offered the clearest and starkest revelation that God is love. He did not try to defend himself against the death sentence; he did not curse his executioners but forgave them; he did not come down from the cross when challenged to do so; he did not use any of his formidable power to save himself from death. It is as if he were saying to us, "Do you see?! I have no power now, none at all. I have relinquished it all out of love for the Father and for you. Do you understand now that God is not power but love?"

God has power, but he can reveal himself without it, for it is not of his essence. However, God can never reveal himself without love, because Love is what God is. The devil, with all of his cunning, does not seem to understand this. And this is why he was outwitted and forever defeated by the passion and death of Jesus.

This mentality of the devil showed itself clearly on Calvary, when the people cried out, "You who would destroy the temple and build it in three days, save yourself! If you are the Son of God, come down from the cross" (Matthew 27:40). The idea that coming down from the cross would give evidence of God's presence makes sense only if God is power. In other words, "If you are the Son of God, then you have to show us your power."

The bystanders' recollection of what Jesus had said about the temple is also telling. They saw the destruction and rebuilding of the temple as an act of power. John reminds us that Jesus was speaking about the temple of his body (see John 2:21). Thus the destruction and rebuilding (the death and resurrection) is not an act of power but an act of love between the Father and the Son and a revelation of the love that the Father and Son have for us. And the love between the Father and the Son is the Holy Spirit. While God loved us at Calvary in a way too profound for words, the devil could see the event only through the prism of power.

When the onlookers tempted Jesus with "If you are the Son of God…," they were repeating the very words of the devil to

Jesus in the desert: "If you are the Son of God, command these stones to become loaves of bread" (Matthew 4:3); "If you are the Son of God, throw yourself down" (Matthew 4:6). Again, the only revelation of God that seems to register with the devil is a demonstration of power.

The apostle Peter had fallen prey to this devilish misconception:

> And [Jesus] began to teach them that the Son of man must suffer many things, and be rejected by the elders and the chief priests and the scribes, and be killed, and after three days rise again. And he said this plainly. And Peter took him, and began to rebuke him. But turning and seeing his disciples, he rebuked Peter, and said, "Get behind me, Satan! For you are not on the side of God, but of men." (Mark 8:31–33)

Peter found it inconceivable that God would submit himself to rejection and death. He thought, as Satan does, that God is power. For Jesus, on the other hand, it is inconceivable not to hand himself over, for he is Love.

In fact, we can see the love of Jesus in the way that he uses his power. In *At the Origin of the Christian Claim*, Monsignor Luigi Giussani points out that Jesus always used his power for good. We, on the other hand, are more accustomed to people who abuse the power that they have: The greater their power, the greater their tendency toward evil. And yet Jesus' power was beyond what anyone had previously seen, and he always used it for good.

Love and Freedom

If you truly love someone, you cannot force that person to reciprocate. The last thing you want to do is take away his or her freedom.

Isn't it interesting that many people accuse God of not showing himself in a way that would force us to recognize him? They are waiting for the manifestation of a God of power, and so they never recognize the one true God who is Love. Isn't it amazing that God, who is the source of everything, never forces himself upon us but invites our freedom? It will always be amazing, because the fact that God is Love is ever new.

It was not only at the cross that Jesus respected our freedom; this occurred throughout his ministry. Recall the rich young man whom Jesus invited to sell everything in order to follow him. It is recounted that Jesus, looking upon him, loved him (Mark 10:21). But when the man went away sad, Jesus did not run after him. Jesus showed the man his love, and the rest was up to the man's freedom. In love Jesus could do no more.

Jesus also loved the scribes and Pharisees who would not follow him. He did all that he could for them, but he could not force them to accept him. One of the most moving scenes in the Gospels is when Jesus weeps over Jerusalem: "O Jerusalem, Jerusalem, killing the prophets and stoning those who are sent to you! How often would I have gathered your children together as a hen gathers her brood under her wings, and you would not!" (Matthew 23:37).

Jesus suffers because of his love for us. He will invite us to the point of humiliation, but he will never force us, because this would not be love. This is not his nature.

In times and places in which members of the Church have forced conversions to Christianity, they have not been acting with the mind of the Church and have, in fact, engaged in a grave sin. Why? Because forcing a conversion is not an act of

WISDOM FOR EVERYDAY LIFE FROM THE BOOK OF REVELATION

love for the person, and since it obscures love, it thus presents an obstacle to a free and true encounter with Christ.

Often in the Rite of Christian Initiation of Adults, I encounter catechized spouses of Catholics who have asked to enter the Church after many years of marriage. Often these catechumens have told me that they always knew that their spouses wanted them to come into the Church, and they were moved by the fact that their spouses never forced the issue. The respect that these men and women received from their wives and husbands attracted them to the Church and witnessed to the God who is Love.

When we look for a god of power, we are not seeking God but running after the devil's deceptive image of God. Perhaps it is for this reason that there is ultimately no neutral ground in the battle. You are loved, and you love truly or you don't—that is, you are with God or against him. True love cannot be faked.

The Hymn of the Virgins

That love cannot be faked is indicated in the encouraging scene that immediately follows the frightful introduction of the first beast and the second beast and the stampings of the mark of the beast. For we now see Jesus, the true Lamb, standing on Mount Zion with his followers, who have his name and his Father's name written on their foreheads. These followers are singing a new song, and "no one could learn that song except the hundred and forty-four thousand who had been redeemed from the earth." (Revelation 14:3).

The fact that God is Love is a living truth that is ever new, and thus the experience of the encounter with Christ cannot be simulated or duplicated without him. Only those Christ has redeemed can learn the song.

According to legend a young singer was brought to audition for Tommy Dorsey. After listening to her, the great bandleader told her agent, "She's a good singer. Bring her back in a few years, after she's really fallen in love and had her heart broken, and then she might be a great singer." The experience of love can't be faked.

And who are these 144,000 redeemed who sing this new song? Most scholars comment that the 144,000 signifies a great multitude and can indicate all of those who follow Christ, as the 144,000 in chapter seven refers to all of the Israelites. Moreover they are virgins. This is not to be taken in a literal physical sense: It is likely a reference to all those who avoided worshiping pagan idols and images, thus all Christians. Monsignor Giussani speaks of virginal love as a love that desires the good destiny of the beloved and is thus a nonpossessive love. It is a love that bears within it a certain detachment from the beloved, in order not to manipulate the beloved as a mere object of one's pleasure.

In the film *The Elephant Man*, the severely deformed John Merrick is reading *Romeo and Juliet* with an actress who visits him. During one visit he tells her that Romeo did not really love Juliet because he gave up on her so quickly. He thinks that Romeo loved the way Juliet made him feel, but he did not really love her. This is a recognition of the difference between virginal love and possessive love.

I used to offer another example to my students. Imagine that a boy is accepted to a great engineering program in Chicago and to one in his home state of New York. He has a full scholarship to each (I told you to *imagine* it!), but the program in Chicago is much better suited to the specialization he would like to pursue. Suppose his mother tells him, "Oh, Honey, don't go to Chicago. I love you too much to have you so far away from me!"

Does this mother really love her son too much? I don't think so. It would seem that if she really loved him, she would allow him to go to the program that is better for him, even at the sacrificial cost of having him far away from her. It seems she doesn't love his destiny but loves the way his presence makes her feel. She somehow wants to possess him.

If this mother succeeds in making her son stay in New York, and if she prevails upon him throughout his life to follow her wishes instead of what he perceives is best for him, she will lose him. He may be physically present to her, but his heart will not be with her. But if she allows him to go to Chicago and freely pursue what is best for him, though she might not see him as often, she will win her son's heart. In refraining from the temptation to possess him, she will truly possess his love.

Thus true love involves a kind of detachment, not one that lessens the love but one that makes the love even greater. It is when we do not have this virginal detachment that true love disappears.

A startlingly extreme example of nonvirginal love is in Ira Levin's *The Stepford Wives*. A group of men love their ideas of what their wives should be and do for them so much that they consent to having their real wives killed in order to replace them with robots.

All Christians, not just those who are called to virginity, are called to love in a virginal way. In an address to the John Paul II Institute in 2001, the pope said, "[V]irginity indicates the final destiny of conjugal love."[4] In the appendix of *Love and*

Responsibility, he speaks of how the marital act is more satisfying for the man and the woman if this kind of virginal love exists in the marriage and informs that act.[5]

Was John Paul II saying that couples should refrain from the marital act? No! Rather that the ideal of married love is that I love my spouse not for the good I receive from him or her but for his or her destiny.

God's Wrath and God's Love

After the vision of the Lamb and his companions, we have three angels. The first angel bears "an eternal gospel to proclaim to those who dwell on earth, to every nation and tribe and tongue and people" (Revelation 14:6). Again we have the theme of the diverse multitude of people invited to hear the gospel; that is, everyone is invited to follow Christ. The second angel speaks of the fall of Babylon the great, which we will come back to in the next chapter (thus following Revelation, which will return to the image of Babylon later on.)

A third angel puts before us the problem of God's wrath and the problem of hell.

> And another angel, a third, followed them, saying with a loud voice, "If any one worships the beast and its image, and receives a mark on his forehead or on his hand, he also shall drink the wine of God's wrath, poured unmixed into the cup of his anger, and he shall be tormented with fire and brimstone in the presence of the holy angels and in the presence of the Lamb. And the smoke of their torment goes up for ever and ever; and they have no rest, day or night, these worshipers of the beast and its image, and whoever receives the mark of its name." (Revelation 14:9–11)

First let us consider the context of the passage. We have just been told that the hour of God's judgment has come (see 14:7). This indicates that we are at the moment when all of our decisions culminate in a final choice. The first angel has announced the good news to all who dwell on earth. Every person has been given what he or she needs in order to make a choice. (Remember, there is no neutrality.)

In each of our lives the Good News has been announced in different ways, and here we are told that the Good News is somehow announced to everyone. It is important to note that the Church teaches that all are saved through Jesus Christ, even if they are not aware of it. Thus a person who loves truly is in relationship with Jesus, because God is love. A person who sincerely seeks the truth is in relationship with Jesus, because he is the Way, the Truth, and the Life.

If, on the other hand, I reject love, if I reject truth, I am rejecting Jesus. The rejection of love and truth will never leave me at peace, and the final and definitive rejection of love and truth will take peace away from me forever.

Those who worship the beast and its image indicate those who choose falsity and deception, even at the point of the final judgment, after the eternal gospel has been proclaimed and offered to them. This seems to be indicated by the text, and it is certainly indicated in the context of the Church. For we know that the ancient Church welcomed back *lapsi*, Christians who out of sin or weakness had worshiped the emperor's image and denied Christ, after they showed sincere repentance. Mercy is offered throughout life and up to the final judgment, but each one of us will freely make a final choice. Our life is a preparation for that final choice.

Thus the fact that eternal torment could exist for those who definitively refuse to accept God's love and truth is not a contradiction to God's love but rather evidence of it. For if God truly loves us, he loves our freedom. In fact, it is his gift of freedom that makes us capable of reciprocating his love. If God is to really respect our freedom, he must respect it to the very end. Because if at the very end union with God is forced upon us, we are not really free.

The possibility of hell must exist if God is love, because we must be free to separate ourselves from him, and in his love he must respect our freedom. And then separation from God becomes its own punishment. In chapter four I mentioned C.S. Lewis's *The Great Divorce,* and I recommend it here as one of the best helps for understanding this problem.

It is also important for us to recognize that anger does not contradict love. If you harm someone I love, I will be angry. The more I love the person, then perhaps the angrier I will be. It is also possible to be angry at a person I love if he is harming himself.

Parents may get angry when their children foolishly or intentionally endanger themselves. They might resort to anger and punishment to point their child on the right path. But there comes a time when parental punishment ceases, and children must decide freely on the direction of their lives. If they choose wrongly, the sufferings that come from those choices will become their own inescapable punishment.

This may offer us some understanding of God's love, which includes wrath and fury, as depicted in the plagues of Revelation 15 and 16. In the letter to Laodicea, Jesus said, "Those whom I love, I reprove and chasten; so be zealous and repent" (Revelation 3:19).

God loves us in the virginal way we spoke of in the previous section. Like the parents of the free child, he might employ punishment and wrath because he has given himself no way of forcing us to be with him. God is not possessive of us. He loves the destiny for which he has made us, because that destiny is union with him. However, he leaves us free, because we cannot reach a destiny of accepting and returning love without our freedom.

In *At the Origin of the Christian Claim*, Monsignor Giussani notes that in his public ministry, Jesus did not begin to go toward the cross until he had revealed himself as clearly as he could to the chosen people of Israel. He waited until those who followed him had reached the conviction they needed, and there was no more he could do to change the position of those who rejected him.[6]

The necessity to make a decision is depicted by the image of "one like a son of man, with a golden crown on his head, and a sharp sickle in his hand" (Revelation 14:14). Jesus reveals himself to us because he loves us, and in loving us he loves our freedom. It is we, with our God-given freedom, who decide on which side of that sharp sickle we will fall.

•

•

•

•

•

CHAPTER SEVEN

Babylon the Harlot and Jerusalem the Bride
Revelation 17—18; 12; 21

When the bowl of the seventh plague is poured out, we read that "God remembered great Babylon, to make her drain the cup of the fury of his wrath" (Revelation 16:19).

We must first note that Babylon was the place of exile for the Jews. After the kingdom of Judah had fallen, around 586 BC, the remaining Jews were exiled to Babylon for what was perhaps their most difficult and confusing moment up to that point. God had promised them a kingdom that would last forever (see 2 Samuel 7), and the fall of Judah and their Babylonian captivity seemed to fly in the face of that promise. In a psalm made popular by pop musicians, the Jews lament their persecution in Babylon:

> By the waters of Babylon,
>   there we sat down and wept,
>   when we remembered Zion.
> On the willows there
>   we hung up our lyres.
> For there our captors
>   required of us songs,

and our tormentors, mirth, saying,
  "Sing us one of the songs of Zion!"

How shall we sing the LORD's song
  in a foreign land?
If I forget you, O Jerusalem,
  let my right hand wither! (Psalm 137:1–5)

Babylon in Revelation seems clearly to be a symbol of Rome, for she is "drunk with the blood of the saints and the blood of the martyrs of Jesus" (Revelation 17:6). For Christians, the new chosen people of God, Rome is the new Babylon, the new foreign land in which they are tormented. While the Jews longed to be freed from Babylon and return to Jerusalem, the Christians seek to be freed from Rome, and they look forward to the New Jerusalem.

God's Beloved and the Devil's Imitation

Babylon is seen in Revelation as a woman, and this is yet another instance in which the devil has shown his lack of originality. It seems that since God has a beloved woman, the devil wants one too. That Babylon is the devil's woman is made clear by the fact that she is seated on top of the beast, specifically the first beast, with his seven heads and ten horns, who has received authority from the dragon. This is the dragon from Revelation 12 who tried to devour the Savior, born of the woman, tried to attack the woman, and then waged war on her offspring.

God clothes his beloved woman with the sun, puts the moon at her feet, and crowns her with twelve stars. The devil has to settle for gold and jewels and pearls, that is, passing riches.

God glorifies his woman and honors her in allowing her to give birth to the son destined to rule the nations. God has prepared a place for this woman, and he cares for her and protects her from the dragon's harm (see 12:14–16). What a contrast to what the devil does for his woman. "And the ten horns that you saw, they and the beast will hate the harlot; they will make her desolate and naked, and devour her flesh and burn her up with fire" (17:16).

Whether she is seen as Mary, Israel, or the Church, God loves the woman of Revelation 12 with a virginal love. He adorns her and gives her glory and rejoices in her.

This imagery continues in the description of the New Jerusalem as the bride of the Lamb (see 19:7–8). God gives his bride life forever; when the New Jerusalem comes down from heaven, there will be no more death (see 21:1–4).

In giving gifts to his beloved, God is not diminished, for the more aware and alive the Church is with the love she has received from God, the more she in turn reflects the glory back to him. When I have a student who is respectful and does well, it makes me think highly of his or her parents.

Mary witnesses to this dynamic of God's love in the Magnificat:

My soul magnifies the Lord,
and my spirit rejoices in God my Savior,
for he has regarded the low estate of his handmaiden.
For behold, henceforth all generations will call me blessed.
(Luke 1:46–48)

When we look at Mary's lowliness and the great graces that God has showered upon her, our understanding and appreciation of God increases. We recognize that he is greater than we thought.

The devil does not understand the paradoxical truth of God's love, and so although Babylon is his woman, seated upon his beast and doing his bidding by drinking the blood of martyrs, the beast ultimately hates her and devours her. He cannot sustain his attempted imitation of God's love, because the devil does not love anyone, even those who participate in his destruction and deceit. In the end, as far as the devil is concerned, it's all about him.

Passing Splendor

Let us now compare the harlot of Babylon to the bride of the Lamb, who is the New Jerusalem. We have already noted that God clothed the woman of Revelation 12 with celestial bodies as opposed to the jewels of the harlot, and God will adorn the bride of the Lamb, the New Jerusalem, with eternal life and his own splendor (see 21:10–11). Interestingly, Babylon also claims unending splendor for herself, "since in her heart she says, 'A queen I sit, I am no widow, mourning I shall never see'" (18:7). And so the merchants that grew rich from her will be shocked at her demise, as they cry out, "What city was like the great city?" (18:18).

Passing riches and passing splendor may claim eternal greatness. Students are often shocked when I tell them that the Roman Empire lasted much longer than the United States has thus far. It seems inconceivable to them that the United States may one day not exist as we know it.

Think of the sports stars, movie stars, rock stars, and political stars who have come and gone in our lifetime. Twenty years ago they seemed like the greatest ever, and now they are mere footnotes, commanding little attention from the old and unknown to the young. Depressions and recessions have also shown us that wealth is not as reliable as we might think. In good economic times people don't see the downturn coming until it is already upon us.

The arrogance of Babylon's claim and the foolishness of the merchants' expectations are answered with the suddenness of her demise. Because she claimed to know no grief, "so shall her plagues come in a single day" (18:8).The merchants marvel that the great city's wealth is ruined in one hour (see 18:17, 19). Think of the United States after 9/11 and after the sudden demise of many banks in 2008.

To place my trust in anything less than the eternal God is to misplace my trust. Outside of him everything passes. But all who are united to him become signs and promises of his eternal splendor.

Compare the Church's two-thousand-year memory of her saints to memories of the great heroes of other realms. The Church begs intercession of her saints with the certainty that they are alive forever; they are not mere heroes of the past. Yes, their earthly lives are over, but those lives carried something of the eternal, and God's eternal splendor has victory over the temporariness of their lives.

Wedded youth comes and goes, but a wedding carries the eternal within. And the New Jerusalem is a bride, while Babylon is only a harlot.

The Bride and the Harlot

When I was a teenager, I had a tremendous crush on Olivia Newton-John. I had two posters in my room, one of the "innocent" Sandy at the beginning of the movie *Grease*, and another of that unfortunate character she devolved into by the end. One day my grandfather came up to my room to smoke (so that my grandmother wouldn't see him). He looked back and forth at the two posters and said to me, "One of 'em you'd want to bring home to meet your mother, the other one looks like you'd better just leave her at a corner in Times Square." (I should note that this was before Times Square was cleaned up.)

The New Jerusalem is a bride; Babylon is a harlot. These images once again bring into relief the difference between the inimitable and lasting love of God and the illusions perpetrated by Satan.

At this point in my high school course on Revelation, I would put "Prostitute" on one side of the blackboard and "Wife" on the other, then have the boys list for me the differences. I was consistently surprised at how seriously the boys took this exercise and how sincerely they would come to the conclusion that a wife is infinitely preferable to the sad prospect of a prostitute. A bride is one who truly loves, who truly wants to give her life to the one she loves, while a harlot is a mockery, a poor imitation of this love. A harlot might go through some superficial motions of a wife, but these are all pretense, and they quickly evaporate into nothingness.

Much of our culture seems to have devolved into harlotry and skeptically given up on the existence of true love. In this climate the Church is frequently blamed for being "against" sex. The truth is that the Church values the marital act much more than any other institution ever has. For within marriage, intercourse is seen as something holy. It is part of the sacrament of marriage to the degree that the marriage is not considered indissoluble until it has been consummated. Every time the man and woman love one another in this way, they renew their marriage vows. For this act is an expression of their promise to give themselves to one another for all of life.

On the other hand, when sexual intercourse is engaged in outside of marriage, it is a sin, because it is not a sign of any such promise. Each person is using the other for pleasure, each reducing the other to an object, even if only for a time. This begins to have effects on the person, not the least of which is doubt that true love exists and perhaps doubt in one's own self-worth.

Sexual expression outside of the marriage covenant, as loving as it may seem, at bottom is a lie. The couple give their bodies over to one another but do not really give themselves.

The Church's teachings on sexuality are not conventional impositions. Rather they are truths concerning the nature of the human person and the love for which we are made. These teachings help us experience and witness to the presence of the true love of God among us and the eternal destiny that this love promises us.

Shortly before her wedding, a friend of mine was talking with a coworker about the new apartment she had found for herself and her soon-to-be husband. Her coworker was shocked to learn that the couple did not live together already. My friend revealed that she and her fiancé had not simulated married life in any way in anticipation of their wedding.

This coworker, who was not a Catholic and apparently not a stranger to marriage simulation, became teary-eyed in front of my friend and told her, "That's beautiful. Good for you! That's how it should be." As alien as it seemed to her, this young woman was attracted to this witness of true love. Our desire for true love cannot be eradicated, and neither can our ability to recognize the difference between true love and illusory imitations of it.

Babylon is full of empty promises, while the New Jerusalem represents the fulfillment for which every human heart longs. The desire of the human heart for the eternal wedding feast of heaven springs from the depths of our human nature.

Beyond the Fall of Babylon

The great multitude of heaven rejoice that Babylon has fallen:

> Hallelujah! Salvation and glory and power belong to our God,
> for his judgments are true and just;
> he has judged the great harlot who corrupted the earth with her
> fornication,
> and he has avenged on her the blood of his servants. (19:1–2)

The next chorus rejoices over the bride and the Lamb:

> Hallelujah! For the Lord our God the Almighty reigns.
> Let us rejoice and exult and give him the glory,
> for the marriage of the Lamb has come,
> and his Bride has made herself ready. (19:6–7)

This is important, because it is not enough that Babylon has fallen. I need the bride and the Lamb to come. Recall Jesus' words in the Gospel of Luke:

> He who is not with me is against me, and he who does not gather with me scatters.
> When the unclean spirit has gone out of a man, he passes through waterless places seeking rest; and finding none he says, "I will return to my house from which I came." And when he comes he finds it swept and put in order. Then he goes and brings seven other spirits more evil than himself, and they enter

and dwell there; and the last state of that man becomes worse than the first. (Luke 11:23–26)

Christianity is not about the absence of evil; it is about the presence of Christ. With no clear and present alternative to the Babylon that has fallen, I will simply fall for the next Babylon.

Think of the colleague of that bride-to-be. Faced with the beauty of chaste love, she was moved. We could even say that for her Babylon fell, because the lies and illusions of the culture in which she lived were momentarily cleared. However, if all she thought was, "Wow, what an upright and traditional and admirable couple," then the moment would fade, and she would return to the Babylon of the New York singles' scene with nothing but the memory of a passing sentiment. If instead she asked why that couple are the way they are, she would be told about a community in the Church that changed that woman and her fiancé because there they recognized Christ. What made that couple different was not their moral strength—that is, the mere freedom from Babylon—but the fact that they had encountered the bride and the Lamb.

In the Woody Allen film *September*, a woman recovering from a breakdown and a suicide attempt is at a summer house with a friend. Toward the end of the summer, the woman attempts suicide again. Her friend loses her temper and tells the woman that she just needs to get back into life, into her job, into hobbies, into meeting new friends, and into the thousand distractions that everyone else finds to keep themselves going. The woman responds, "Don't you see? I don't want to die; I want to live. But all anyone can offer me is a thousand distractions."

We need someone or something to live for. The solution offered young people to "Just Say No" is useless if there is not something to say yes to. If moralism was enough, then Jesus would likely have been pleased with the Pharisees.

If the Church in the United States in the '40s and '50s was so great, then how did the '60s and '70s happen? When the culture proposed drugs, sex, rock and roll, contraception, divorce, and freedom from responsibility, it seems that many Catholics followed along. The exodus of priests and religious makes you wonder why those men and women had entered upon those vocations in the first place. Had there been a true encounter with Christ? Was Christ palpably present in those religious communities, or was there nothing proposed other than a form of life? Had the Church been reduced to a moral teacher with a formal and orderly structure?

When you lose Christ, you ultimately lose an attraction that calls out to the human heart. The house can look clean and tidy, but if Christ is not clearly present, it is not attractive, and it will fall before the allure of Babylon.

Jesus brings us the value and truth of virginity, the sacramental value of faithfulness in marriage, and many other good things. What we often fail to realize is that those good things cannot be sustained without him. An upright, traditional, admirable life is not sustainable without Christ, because it is not enough to satisfy the human heart, which as Saint Augustine said, is restless until it rests in God.[1]

In fact, when we love the Church merely for its moral teachings, its traditions, or its structures, without seeking Christ himself, then we are loving Jesus in a nonvirginal way. We can reduce Christ to the externals of his body, the Church, just as a "lover" might "love" the body of his beloved but not the person. We might look like the bride, but we are just another harlot.

The Pelagians thought they could live morally without Christ. Saint Augustine told them that this was the horrendous and hidden virus of their heresy, that they claimed to make the grace of Christ consist in his example and not in his gift of himself.[2]

Look back at the first letter that Jesus wrote to the seven churches, the letter to Ephesus (see Revelation 2:1–7). Jesus recognizes and commends the patient endurance of the Ephesians and their avoidance of evil. But he tells them that they have lost the love they had at first, and thus they have fallen.

It is not enough for any of us to escape from Babylon. We need Jerusalem. We need to become members of the bride, who is destined for fulfillment through her union with the Lamb.

•

•

•

•

•

CHAPTER EIGHT

The Final Victory: The Marriage of Jesus
and His Church
Revelation 19—21

After the heavenly multitude rejoice at the fall of Babylon and the arrival of the wedding day of the Lamb, John tells us:

> Then I saw heaven opened, and behold, a white horse! He who sat upon it is called Faithful and True, and in righteousness he judges and makes war. His eyes are like a flame of fire, and on his head are many diadems; and he has a name inscribed which no one knows but himself. He is clothed in a robe dipped in blood, and the name by which he is called is The Word of God. And the armies of heaven, wearing fine linen, white and pure, followed him on white horses. (Revelation 19:11–14)

We have mentioned already that Jesus refers to himself in Revelation as the Alpha and the Omega (see 1:8). At the opening of the first seal, he is the first to emerge riding on a white horse, and now he appears again as the events of the final seal reach their climax. His fiery eyes remind us of John's description of him at the beginning of Revelation. His robe is dipped in blood, recalling his death, and he is called The Word of God, which is what John the evangelist calls Jesus at the beginning of his Gospel.

Unlike the first time we saw Jesus on a white horse, this time he is not alone. "The armies of heaven, wearing fine linen, white and pure, followed him on white horses" (19:14). Recall that in the letter to Sardis, Jesus wrote,

> Yet you have still a few names in Sardis, people who have not soiled their garments; and they shall walk with me in white, for they are worthy. He who conquers shall be clothed like them in white garments, and I will not blot his name out of the book of life. (3:4–5)

This army is dressed in the same garment as the bride, of "fine linen, bright and pure" (19:8).

Jesus is surrounded by the victors who remain with him, his followers, his bride, the Church. It seems that Christians truly are waiting for a knight on a white horse to come and take us away! And any other knight who claims to be the one we are waiting for truly is an illusion, as from a fairy tale or, more accurately, a horror story.

It is also interesting that his followers, like Jesus, are on white horses. They kind of look like him. They are, in a sense, "other Christs." John refers to this mystery in his first letter: "Beloved, we are God's children now; it does not yet appear what we shall be, but we know that when he appears we shall be like him, for we shall see him as he is" (1 John 3:2).

As I mentioned in chapter two, John had personal experience of this. The Acts of the Apostles speaks of his being arrested with Peter and brought before the Sanhedrin, just as Jesus had been. And we are told that the interrogators, "when they saw the boldness of Peter and John, and perceived that they were uneducated, common men, ... wondered; and they recognized that they had been with Jesus" (Acts 4:13). The

Sanhedrin recognized that Peter and John had been with Jesus not because they remembered seeing their faces before but because Peter and John, in their boldness, were like Jesus.

A Quick Victory

And I saw the beast and the kings of the earth with their armies gathered to make war against him who sits upon the horse and against his army. (Revelation 19:19)

Remember at the beginning of our study, when I mentioned that all of Revelation was leading up to a final battle? Well, here it is. This is the moment we have been waiting for. This is the moment of confrontation. Let's see how it plays out.

And the beast was captured, and with it the false prophet who in its presence had worked the signs by which he deceived those who had received the mark of the beast and those who worshiped its image. These two were thrown alive into the lake of fire that burns with brimstone. And the rest were slain by the sword of him who sits upon the horse, the sword that issues from his mouth; and all the birds were gorged with their flesh. (19:20–21)

Is that it? Is that all? The entire battle is over in two verses! Jesus simply throws the two beasts into the fire and then kills the rest of the army with his sword, seemingly in one fell swoop.

My students would sometimes get annoyed with me because this is not the epic Hollywood battle they thought they were being set up for. Their mistake, and the mistake that many of us make, is to think that the devil is a match for God.

There is one Hollywood battle that does seem similar to this quick victory. In *Raiders of the Lost Ark*, when Indiana Jones is confronted with a frightening swordsman, it seems that it is all over for him. Yet he calmly looks at the frightening figure, who is slowly and threateningly approaching him, takes out his gun, shoots him, and then continues on his way. The devil is kind of like that swordsman: He seems really scary, but before the presence of Jesus, there is not much to him. (An analogy that makes Indiana Jones into a Christ figure may limp a bit, but it comes in very handy in a classroom at a boys' school on an eighty-seven-degree June day.)

Now, what about Jesus' army? What did they do?

When I would ask the students this question, the answer invariably would be "nothing." I would ask them again and again until one student would suddenly have a "eureka" face and blurt out, "They were with Jesus!"

The army didn't do much fighting. They were victors, they were conquerors, because they simply stayed with Jesus, just as he had advised them to do in those seven letters. In John's Gospel Jesus said, "Apart from me you can do nothing" (John 15:5). The John of Revelation, with this vision of victory, assures us that with Jesus we can conquer.

Earlier we noted that we don't look at the saints of the Church the way nations might look at their heroes. Saints did not succeed with their own strength; they are men and women of the Church who continually begged for Jesus and stayed with him and depended on him. This dependence is a common thread that runs through the life of every true saint, canonized and otherwise.

The army and the bride are one. They are victorious precisely because of their longing for the Groom and their desire to stay with him.

Harbingers of Victory

The devil might seem like a formidable foe, but he is really nothing when put up against God. In "Choruses from 'The Rock,'" T.S. Eliot writes, "But the man who is will shadow / The man that pretends to be."[1] Revelation shows us that Jesus, the God who is, always shadows the devil, who is the god pretending to be. Let us look at two passages in John's Gospel to see what this means.

Consider first the Samaritan woman who encounters Jesus at the well (see John 4). She has had five husbands, and she is living with a sixth man, to whom she is not married. She must be accustomed to overtures of love that turn out to be empty. In a relatively brief conversation at the well, she is completely taken by the love that Jesus gives.

Jesus is rather blunt toward her, but it is clear that he has waited specifically for her at that well and is concerned for her person in a way that none of her husbands have been. Here now is a man who loves her in a nonpossessive and true way. He loves her for her, not for his advantage. This love sends her running into town to tell everyone about this man.

Next consider the blind man whom Jesus heals in John 9. In order to discredit the miracle, the Pharisees call the man before them and bear down upon him with all the threat their position and authority can muster. Even the man's parents crumble before the Pharisees. The man, however, is unconquerable. He keeps repeating what Jesus did for him, and the Pharisees cannot trip him up. The man has experienced the true authority of Jesus, after which the Pharisees' display of "authority" is as nothing. In fact, it is the Pharisees who crumble before the healed man. In the end all they can do before his certainty is call him a sinner and throw him out.

In Mark's Gospel there is a Roman soldier who comes to believe in Jesus by watching him die: "When the centurion, who stood facing him, saw that he thus breathed his last, he said, 'Truly this man was the Son of God!'" (Mark 15:39). Think about this man. All around him people are mocking Jesus and implying that he is an impostor. The soldier is not even from the chosen people, who were expecting a Messiah. However, in looking at the way Jesus dies, he recognizes all the hate-filled commotion around him to be false and Jesus to be true.

The centurion has probably seen many crucifixions before. The dying criminals must have either pathetically begged for pity or cursed up a storm, having nothing more to lose. But this centurion sees Jesus praying for his persecutors and asking God to forgive them.

We can recognize the same dynamic in the good thief, whom Luke presents (see Luke 23:39–43). In the midst of all the lies swirling around Jesus, lies that are coming from some very authoritative figures, the thief recognizes the truth. The authority of the Pharisees is as nothing before the authority of Jesus, who abandons himself with great certainty into the hands of the Father.

The cross is perhaps the supreme paradigm of Jesus' victory over the devil. While the devil bears down upon Jesus with all the strength of his hate and his threats, Jesus' victory is happening. He defeats the empty show of power (see Colossians 2:15) with the love he has for his Father and for his Father's children, even those who are killing him! The soldier and the thief witness the attractiveness of Jesus' victory, not at the resurrection but already present right there on the cross. May all

of us one day sit confidently on white horses next to that soldier and that thief—next to Jesus.

Harbingers of Defeat

If the Samaritan woman, the healed blind man, the soldier, and
the thief show us what victory looks like, who are examples of
defeat? Who would want to be in the army of the beast, which
fights against Jesus?

The Pharisees who were harassing the healed blind man certainly looked like the beast. They wanted the man to lie about
what had happened to him in order to reinforce their lies about
Jesus. These were lies that those Pharisees were telling not only
the people but also themselves. They must have noticed the
exceptionality of Jesus, just as everyone else did. However, in
their stubbornness and pride, they would not accept the Word
of God who had become flesh. Perhaps they preferred the
Word of God to remain a slave to their interpretations.

Jesus disparaged the Pharisees not only for their own hardness of heart but also for the fact that they infected others:
"Woe to you, scribes and Pharisees, hypocrites! for you tra-
verse sea and land to make a single proselyte, and when he
becomes a proselyte, you make him twice as much a child of
hell as yourselves" (Matthew 23:15).

We see evidence of this after the raising of Lazarus: "Many
of the Jews …, who had come with Mary and had seen what he
did, believed in him; but some of them went to the Pharisees
and told them what Jesus had done" (John 11:45–46). Imagine
the hardness of these people's hearts. They have just seen Jesus
raise a man from the dead! The greatest problem of human life
has just been conquered by a man claiming to be the Son of

God, and instead of responding to the attraction of such a momentous event, all they can think about is telling the Pharisees about Jesus' latest breach of religious etiquette. Their involvement in the Pharisees' battle against Jesus blinds them to the promise of Jesus' very presence.

I was once called a "Pharisee" on a priests' retreat. I had gotten so upset over some minor changes in the way the retreat was being conducted that I risked overlooking the miracle of the unity of the priests participating and the hope that Christ was awakening in all of us. Thankfully I had a friend who loved me enough to call me a Pharisee. I also catch my pharisaical jealousy when I see Christ working in ways that are not according to my preconceptions or moving people in ways that I don't expect.

Have you had the experience of having someone offend you and repent, then finding yourself a bit angry at the freedom they enjoy in Christ, which goes against your petty sense of justice? We can connive with a devilish anger when we see how much Jesus loves someone against whom we are nursing a grudge.

The army of the beast is not made up of aliens; it is made up of hardened human hearts. We all have connived with the beast and perhaps helped him in his heinous fight. Our hope is that Jesus continues to send us "letters" to awaken us to our sinfulness and foolishness.

If you find a friend who loves you enough to correct you when you are "going to the other side," then stay with that friend. Follow that friend; he is a letter from Jesus in the flesh. Follow him right up to your white horse, where you will be with Jesus, who is the origin and destiny of all friendship.

Jesus offered his friendship to all the Pharisees. In the end there will not be a single member of the army of the beast who has not, in some way, been offered the friendship of Jesus. But they will have preferred their own ways and strategies of living (even of following God) to that of following a friend who loves them and knows them better than they love and know themselves.

We have heard the expression "If you don't stand for something, you will fall for anything." In the end, if you don't stand with Jesus, you will fall into the illusion of following yourself. Why is it an illusion? Because in rejecting Jesus you will inevitably make something less than the one true God into your god. You will be ready to give ultimate value to whatever the current powerful influences of your culture are assigning ultimate value.

In chasing after a false god or making your own ideas into your god, you are not original at all: You look just like that beast. You are a harbinger of your own defeat. When, on the other hand, you allow Christ to defeat your petty and prideful ideas, you become a harbinger of the ultimate victory.

The Thousand-Year Reign

After the quick victory over the first and second beasts and their army, which concludes chapter nineteen, chapter twenty gives us the somewhat difficult image of the thousand-year reign. The devil is bound up for a thousand years, while those who have been beheaded for their witness come to life and reign with Jesus. After those thousand years the devil will be released for a short time to mislead the nations, and then Jesus will consume the devil's minions with fire and throw him into the pool of fire, where he will be tormented along with the two beasts forever and ever.

Is this thousand-year reign to be taken literally? Is it something that happens in heaven or on earth?

Then I saw an angel coming down from heaven, holding in his hand the key of the bottomless pit and a great chain. And he seized the dragon, that ancient serpent, who is the Devil and Satan, and bound him for a thousand years, and threw him into the pit, and shut it and sealed it over him, that he should deceive the nations no more, till the thousand years were ended. After that he must be let out for a little while.

Then I saw thrones, and seated on them were those to whom judgment was committed. Also I saw the souls of those who had been beheaded for their testimony to Jesus and for the word of God, and who had not worshiped the beast or its image and had not received its mark on their foreheads or their hands. They came to life, and reigned with Christ a thousand years. The rest of the dead did not come to life until the thousand years were ended. This is the first resurrection. Blessed and holy is he who shares in the first resurrection! Over such the second death has no power, but they shall be priests of God and of Christ, and they shall reign with him a thousand years.

And when the thousand years are ended, Satan will be released from his prison and will come out to deceive the nations which are at the four corners of the earth, that is, Gog and Magog, to gather them for battle; their number is like the sand of the sea. And they marched up over the broad earth and surrounded the camp of the saints and the beloved city; but fire came down from heaven and consumed them, and the devil who had deceived them was thrown into the lake of fire and brimstone where the beast and the false prophet were, and they will be tormented day and night for ever and ever. (Revelation 20:1–10)

It would seem impossible to take this passage literally. It may be referring to the life in heaven before the final judgment, in which case it would be hard to posit a literal thousand years. How do you speak of time in a life that is beyond time? Who are the "rest of the dead" who don't come to life until the end of the thousand years? Does the "first resurrection" refer to the ones who were beheaded and came to life or to the rest, who came to life after the thousand years? I happily invoke my admission in the preface that I would not explain each and every image and symbol of Revelation.

I will say, however, that a very helpful reflection on this passage is given by Donal McIlraith in *Everyone's Apocalypse*. Father McIlraith warns against trying to interpret this passage too literally, and he follows the interpretation of Saint Augustine that the thousand years is a symbol for the time between the first and second comings of Christ. It is the time of the Church.[2]

In looking at it this way, the first resurrection can be seen as baptism. Perhaps then, being beheaded for witness to Christ can be seen as the dying and rising that we go through in baptism. It could also refer to the dying and rising that every true Christian will go through in the many conversions that must occur throughout his or her lifetime.

The notion here is that the encounter with Jesus Christ gives me a foretaste of eternal life, here and now. My experience of life in Christ limits the power of the devil over me. Christ present in my life continually provides an attractive and true alternative to the emptiness of the devil.

The thousand years of reigning with Christ are much greater than the "little while" of the devil. Perhaps we again have the theme of the lasting love of Christ as compared to the brief and passing illusion of the devil and his temptations. That there is nothing behind the devil's deceitful pomp is shown with a second quick victory. The devil is thrown into the pool of fire with the same swift ease as were the first and second beasts.

The Books

> I saw the dead, great and small, standing before the throne, and books were opened. Also another book was opened, which is the book of life. And the dead were judged by what was written in the books, by what they had done. (Revelation 20:12)

We have already discussed the images of the scrolls: the scroll with seven seals in Revelation 5 and the one little scroll given to John in Revelation 10. Recall that the scroll with the seals is an image of the one great history of salvation, and each person has a small scroll or book, detailing his or her role in that history. My scroll is my own, my role is my own, and I am responsible for it. No one can shirk his or her responsibility or downplay its significance.

Notice that both the great and the small are before the throne: Both Joan of Arc, who led armies, and Thérèse of Lisieux, who never left her convent; both the rich young man and the poor old widow. For not all popes and kings are saints, and not all saints are popes and kings; God's measure is not our measure.

I was moved at the funeral of Monsignor Luigi Giussani when Cardinal Tettamanzi kept referring to him as a "priest of Milan." He was not a bishop and not a pope, but this "priest of Milan" spread knowledge and affection for Christ throughout the world.

Our individual lives, our individual yeses to Christ, build up the Church and the world in ways we cannot always see and could never measure. As Mary's yes brought Christ into the world for all time, our yeses magnify Christ's presence, and our nos obscure it. There is no neutral position. The decision not to decide for Christ is a decision, and it has an effect on history, and those who decide not to decide will be held fully accountable for that decision.

The image of the scrolls also shows us the way that God loves us. He does not love the billions of men and women he has created as some kind of massively beautiful conglomeration. He doesn't love us all as we might love beautiful beach sand. He loves each of us personally. He sees into the infinite depths of each one of us with a love we cannot imagine. The Book of Life is a unity of individual books that recount yeses said to God from myriad backgrounds, temperaments, times, places, and circumstances.

Paul reminds us that together we make up the one body of Christ, and no one member can be discounted:

> For just as the body is one and has many members, and all the members of the body, though many, are one body, so it is with Christ. For by one Spirit we were all baptized into one body—Jews or Greeks, slaves or free—and all were made to drink of one Spirit.
>
> For the body does not consist of one member but of many. If the foot should say, "Because I am not a hand, I do not belong to the body," that would not make it any less a part of the body. And if the ear should say, "Because I am not an eye, I do not belong to the body," that would not make it any less a part of the body. If the whole body were an eye, where would be the hearing? If the whole body were an ear, where would be the

sense of smell? But as it is, God arranged the organs in the body, each one of them, as he chose. If all were a single organ, where would the body be? As it is, there are many parts, yet one body. The eye cannot say to the hand, "I have no need of you," nor again the head to the feet, "I have no need of you." On the contrary, the parts of the body which seem to be weaker are indispensable, and those parts of the body which we think less honorable we invest with the greater honor, and our unpresentable parts are treated with greater modesty, which our more presentable parts do not require. But God has so composed the body, giving the greater honor to the inferior part, that there may be no discord in the body, but that the members may have the same care for one another. If one member suffers, all suffer together; if one member is honored, all rejoice together.

Now you are the body of Christ and individually members of it. (1 Corinthians 12:12–27)

We "are the body of Christ and individually members of it." Our union is complete, but it is not like the union of drops of water that are lost in the ocean. We are completely united to Christ, and in this union we don't lose ourselves but gain ourselves. This is the unity for which we have been made and without which we are incomplete. It is perhaps an echo of the mystery of the Trinity, in which three persons are one God.

It is also a fulfillment of the mystery of the sacrament of marriage, in which the two become one. And so we come to the great marriage feast of Revelation. It is the marriage between Christ and his Church.

The Wedding of the Lamb

Before a wedding can take place in the Church, there is a lot of preparation and a lot of paperwork. The couple need to verify that their life together up to this point warrants the permanent union of marriage, and the paperwork verifies that there are no obstacles to this union. The scrolls of Revelation verify that preparation has occurred and that union with the Lamb is warranted. "And I saw the holy city, new Jerusalem, coming down out of heaven from God, prepared as a bride adorned for her husband" (Revelation 21:2).

All of salvation history leads to this wedding; every human heart longs for this union. Perhaps the weddings that conclude so many fairy tales and romantic movies are echoes of this persistent human desire and vocation. Weddings are among the most revered rituals of many cultures. Something deep within us knows that we are destined for a wedding in which we will finally reach the completion for which we long. The dominant image of heaven is a wedding feast, even though Jesus said that in heaven we neither marry nor are given in marriage (see Matthew 22:30; Mark 12:25).

The wedding in heaven is the wedding of the Church, the bride, with Jesus, the Bridegroom. This is the heavenly wedding of which every earthly marriage is an image or foreshadowing. Before the ultimate union with Jesus, the marriages that are signs of that union are no longer necessary. The mystery is that this will not be the nullification of all that couples enjoy in their married lives but rather the fulfillment of it.

At the moment of the bride's appearance, John tells us, "the sea was no more" (Revelation 21:1). For ancient peoples the sea was a place of uncertainty and danger. Who knew what lurked beneath those waters? How many seamen left shore never to be seen or heard from again? How did they disappear? What kind of death did they die?

This sinister image of the sea is also reflected in the visions of Revelation. Recall that after the woman escaped from the dragon at the end of chapter twelve, the dragon took up its position on the sand of the sea (see 12:17). Then the first beast rose out of the sea (13:1).

Now the sea is no more. This would seem to signify that there is no more fear of danger or death. No unexpected evil can compromise the union that is about to come into being.

As joyful as an earthly marriage might be, death threatens its duration. Even before death the sin of the spouses can cast doubt upon their union. No marriage is perfect. We see this in the Church's wedding rite: As soon as the spouses have exchanged their vows, the priest prays, "May the Lord in his goodness strengthen your consent." It is as if the Church is asking God to make up for the weakness in the vows, a weakness that will always be there because of original sin.

Recall that the first manifestation of original sin in Adam and Eve is that they realized they were naked and clothed themselves. They did this before the Lord came back into the garden. This means that they were ashamed even in front of each other. There were aspects of themselves that they held back and hid from one another. Their unity was compromised.

The wedding of the New Jerusalem with the Lamb is total. It has none of this weakness or uncertainty and will never be threatened by sin or death, for "death shall be no more" (Revelation 21:4). This is the perfect union to which holy yet imperfect earthly marriages point.

Husband and Wife, Parent and Child

Monsignor Giussani once said to me that relationships between spouses and between parents and children are echoes of what is happening in God. Interestingly, after we hear about the New Jerusalem, "prepared as a bride adorned for her husband" (Revelation 21:2), and before the holy city is called "the wife of the Lamb" (21:9), the one who sits on the throne says, "He who conquers shall have this heritage, and I will be his God and he shall be my son" (Revelation 21:7). In the midst of wedding imagery, we have father-son imagery.

It seems as if our adoption as sons and daughters is fulfilled in the wedding with Jesus, the Lamb. As your child's spouse becomes like a son or daughter to you, so our marriage with Jesus makes us sons and daughters of the Father. So just as earthly marriages are images and prophecies of the promised union of Christ and his Church, relationships of parents and children are images of our relationship with God.

We noted in the introduction to this book that Revelation has to do not just with the future but also with the present. So what does the fact that these family relationships point to and are fulfilled in heaven have to do with my life on earth? How is God's will borne out on earth as it is in heaven?

When I recognize my spouse or my children or my parents as signs of God's eternal love, it changes the way I relate to them. The same could be said about close friends who become like family members to me. (Jesus, after all, refers to us as brothers and sisters who are children of the same heavenly Father.) It is true that relationships in this life are wounded and frequently compromised by sin. But if I recognize these relationships as bearers of God's love, I don't stop at the wounds. I look beyond them. I recognize that the relationships have infinite value, immeasurably greater than the wounds that sin and division inflict.

Think of the resurrection appearances in John's Gospel. When Jesus appeared to the disciples, he showed them his wounds, and "the disciples were glad when they saw the Lord" (John 20:20). The wounds were remnants of the violent death that Jesus suffered as a result of sin, but this didn't stop the joy of the disciples. The Risen Jesus redeemed the wounds, and thus the wounds did not compromise the disciples' joy but rather somehow enhanced it and made it truer.

Before the resurrected Jesus revealed himself to them, John and Peter had been at the empty tomb. John ran and arrived at the tomb first, but he stopped and waited for Peter to enter the tomb before him (see John 20:5–6). Think carefully about this moment.

John knows that Peter was not at the cross, as he promised Jesus he would be. Peter may not have told John about his betrayals, but John knows Peter well, and he sees that he is deeply regretful. Understand, then, the redemptive beauty of John's gesture. How John must want to enter and see, but he waits in deference to Peter. In that respectful pause John says, "Peter, my friend, I know you broke your promise, and I know you are ashamed, but you are not Peter the betrayer. You are Peter chosen by Christ as the rock on which he will build his Church; you are Peter chosen to pray for the rest of us and bring us together after we were scattered by Satan. Your betrayal is redeemed and outshone by the infinite significance given you by the love and mercy of Christ."

John's gaze upon Peter was an experience of the redemption of the Risen Christ, which occurred even before either of them had seen his risen flesh. When we gaze upon one another as John gazed upon Peter, we experience the eternal wedding feast of heaven well before we finally arrive there.

A couple I know suffered a difficult time in the early years of their marriage. Their young relationship quickly became tainted by hurts and serious betrayals, and at the low point of that time, they agreed that they could not remain together. But as they began to take concrete steps toward separation and divorce, they both began to experience serious regret. They knew that there was much more to the history and substance of their marriage than the failures, many though they were. They prayed and sought out a marriage counselor who respected and understood the sacramentality of their marriage. And with their eyes on the fact that Christ was the substance of their marriage, they were able to experience the love of Christ and allow that to save their marriage.

Years later the couple told me that they were happy for their early difficulties, painful as they had been. Those difficulties, which demanded so much repentance and forgiveness, made them aware of their need for mercy, whose name is Jesus. They didn't stop at the wounds! They recognized Christ. They now continue to live the experience of heaven's eternal wedding feast in the midst of their earthly and imperfect marriage.

When my older sister was about to begin her first day of kindergarten, my father gave her an acorn pin and said to her, "May this acorn one day grow into a great tree, and may your life grow to be great." My sister wore that pin every year on the first day of school. Even in high school, when she "hated" my father, she pinned that pin onto her Grateful Dead jacket. She also wore it on her wedding dress.

(Note: Isn't it interesting how important the father-daughter relationship becomes on her wedding day? Here is a simple expression of the wedding feast of heaven, in which Jesus becomes Groom to the Church, and God becomes her Father!)

What does that acorn pin signify? That my father's love for my sister has a deep and eternal foundation, deeper than whatever fights or shortcomings have threatened to eclipse the eternal love of God the Father that is contained in that relationship.

In a time when divorce is prevalent and it is fashionable to begrudge our parents for their real or perceived failures, faithful Christians witness to the eternal wedding feast of the bride and the Lamb, in which we become sons and daughters of God. We witness to this by not stopping at the wounds. Every time we look beyond the sins and betrayals of those whom God has given to us, look more profoundly to the divine and foundational love contained in those relationships, and allow this truer gaze to enkindle in us the burning desire for mercy and reconciliation, we bear witness to the eternal wedding of Christ and his Church. This we know is in our future because we already experience it in the present. Life on earth is lived more truly and adequately when we recognize that it already contains the seeds of our heavenly fulfillment.

Life-Giving Water and the Tree of Life

The life-giving water mentioned in Revelation 21:6 is reminiscent of the life-giving water Jesus promises the Samaritan woman at the well in the Gospel of John: "Whoever drinks of the water that I shall give him will never thirst; the water that I shall give him will become in him a spring of water welling up to eternal life" (John 4:14).

It is interesting that life-giving water is promised in Revelation in the midst of the wedding feast. In the Old Testament there seems to be a connection between wells and marriage. Abraham's servant found Rebekah, the future wife of Isaac, at a well (see Genesis 24), and Moses met his wife, Zipporah, at a well (see Exodus 2:15–21).

Jesus' encounter with the Samaritan woman at the well also seems to contain marriage imagery. The woman is living with a sixth man, who is not her husband. If we recall that six seems to be a number of imperfection, it would make sense that "husband" number six was not even a real husband but a poor imitation. Who is Jesus? He is number seven! He is the fulfillment of what the woman has been desiring and lacking in all the husbands that precede this meeting at the well. This meeting of Jesus and the Samaritan is a prophecy of the wedding feast for which we are all destined.

As Jesus is the Groom infinitely beyond all earthly grooms and the fulfillment toward which they point, life-giving water is much more desirable than well water, for which you must always return and which never completely satisfies. The revelation of the Bridegroom goes hand in hand with the promise of life-giving water that springs up eternally. Revelation 22:1 tells us that the source of this life-giving water is the throne of God and of the Lamb. Here the life-giving water gives rise to the Tree of Life.

After Adam and Eve fell in Genesis, they were separated not only from one another (recall the shame they felt before one another) but also from the Tree of Life. As a result of this insurmountable alienation, every relationship of love in this world would be threatened and seemingly annihilated by death. Faced with the death of a loved one, especially a spouse, a parent, or a child, our longing for the Tree of Life and our sense of its inaccessibility are perhaps most intense.

In the new heaven, after the perfect wedding has been consummated, the Tree of Life is no longer guarded but stands on either side of the river, and its leaves are medicine for the nations: That is, everyone in the holy city or the new heaven seems to have access. True and complete union with Jesus, the New Adam, brings eternal life and healing. The union can never be compromised, and shame will be no more.

Christian tradition often has seen the cross of Christ as the Tree of Life. John writes of the water and blood that flow from the side of Christ as he hangs upon the tree (see John 19:33–34). This water and blood have been seen as the birth of the Church. As Eve came from the side of Adam, the Church is born from the side of Christ.

In the water from Christ's side, the Church has seen an image of baptism; in the blood from the side of Christ, the Church has seen an image of the Eucharist; and when Christ is seen as a New Adam from which the Church is born, as Eve was born from Adam's side, we have an image of marriage. All the sacraments we receive point to and promise the eternal consummation that is expressed in the consummate vision of Revelation.

God Is the Light; the Lamb Is the Lamp

And the city has no need of sun or moon to shine upon it, for the glory of God is its light, and its lamp is the Lamb. (Revelation 21:23)

And night shall be no more; they need no light of lamp or sun, for the Lord God will be their light, and they shall reign for ever and ever. (Revelation 22:5)

In the new heaven and new earth, God is everything. There is no need for a lesser object like the sun or moon to give light, because God is the light. There is no need for wells, because life-giving water comes from God and from the Lamb. There is no need for marriages between God's children, for Jesus is the Bridegroom.

Often we hear someone in love tell us that his beloved is "everything," or we might hear a parent describe a child as "everything." It seems that we are always looking for someone or something that can be everything to us. Giussani writes that we are always "affirming the reality of an 'ultimate.' For by the very fact that he lives five minutes [man] affirms the existence of a 'something' which deep down makes living those five minutes worthwhile."[3]

However, no created being, even a spouse or a child, and no imagined goal, no matter how lofty, is sufficient to be our everything. In the heavenly city God reveals himself as the everything for which we have always longed. He is truly our everything who will never die or disappoint or be found partial or inadequate. We don't need any other light, because God is the light.

What does this say for me today, in the "old" earth? It reminds me that nothing short of the infinite God can be the foundation of my life.

Often we place our hopes in our reductive and immature images of what will make us happy. My hope is in the stability of my job, or my hope is in the success of my children, or my hope is in the solutions promised by a politician or political party. Even as Christians we can set aside Christ as a "spiritual add-on" to our lives and put our real hope in something else.

Notice some of those who do not participate in the wedding

feast of the new heaven: murderers, fornicators, sorcerers, idolaters, and all liars (see Revelation 21:8). Murderers, sorcerers, and liars place their hopes in their own schemes. They want to dictate what reality should be according to their ideas; they will not accept life and circumstances as given by God. Fornicators and idolaters stop on something short of God and make that their everything.

The new heaven is already present now, and I can see it more clearly when I place my hope in God, when he is my light and I do not place my hope in anything less.

•

•

•

•

•

Come, Lord Jesus!

We must not forget that the ultimate wedding celebration, which ushers in the new heaven and earth, occurs at the end of a battle with Satan. Satan wanted to make God nothing and himself everything. He did not accept the love of God but settled for his distorted imitations of that love. This led Satan to nothingness.

The bride of the Lamb recognizes that without Christ she can do nothing. She makes God her everything, and this leads her to eternal life. This is the daily drama of the Christian, and it involves a struggle between a lie and the truth.

You don't get invited to a wedding out of the blue. You are invited as a result of your relationship and familiarity with the bride or the groom. I want to become familiar with Christ in this life. This means that I must continually verify that the actions that Christ takes in my life, through that part of the Church and that part of the world in which he has placed me, are what bring me happiness here and now.

This life is a courtship. Jesus the Bridegroom is wooing us. All of life is a decision, a preparation to say yes to the Bridegroom at the final fulfillment, when he makes his ultimate proposal of marriage.

Our nature is to expect. We have a sense that happiness is promised to us. This is why we get upset when bad things happen. There is something in us that says we are supposed to be happy. Everyone has this expectation; it is a human characteristic. So much so that we know that to give up on it would make us less human.

This is why even the secular world will look to grief counselors when tragedies occur. No matter how horrible the tragedy, to allow a person to lose hope in life seems to be universally abhorrent. Human expectation and hope cannot be stopped.

Revelation ends by exalting and clarifying this expectation: "Come, Lord Jesus." You see, happiness has a name. The beauty, the peace, the justice, the harmony, and the truth for which every human being longs have a name: Jesus.

Christians are not those who have their heads in the clouds; they are the ones who are most aware of their longing and most familiar with the answer to their longing: Jesus. "The Spirit and the Bride say, 'Come.' And let him who hears say, 'Come.' And let him who is thirsty come, let him who desires take the water of life without price" (Revelation 22:17).

Everyone thirsts; everyone wants. The Christian is the one who has found what he or she *really* desires, *really* thirsts for, and is not fooled by anything less.

But even having found Jesus, we are at a loss because he indeed is infinite. He is the life-giving water that springs up eternally, a water we can experience but never exhaust or fully comprehend. Without him we can do nothing, and so we cannot even follow him and remain faithful to him and to our God-given desires without his continual help. We even have difficulty asking for him without our asking being clouded by our own images and schemes.

And so Christ gives us the Spirit. Note that it is the Spirit and the Bride who say, "Come." Saint Paul explains:

> We know that the whole creation has been groaning with labor pains together until now; and not only the creation, but we ourselves, who have the first fruits of the Spirit, groan inwardly as we wait for adoption as sons, the redemption of our bodies. For in this hope we were saved. Now hope that is seen is not hope. For who hopes for what he sees? But if we hope for what we do not see, we wait for it with patience.
>
> Likewise the Spirit helps us in our weakness; for we do not know how to pray as we ought, but the Spirit himself intercedes for us with sighs too deep for words. (Romans 8:22–26)

God and the Lamb truly give us everything by giving us the Spirit. For the Spirit hopes and asks with us, and the Spirit knows the One who is the object of our hope and our asking, in a way too profound for words.

John, the beloved disciple, inspired by the Spirit, concludes the book of Revelation with perhaps the greatest articulation of our reason to have hope.

> He who testifies to these things says, "Surely I am coming soon." Amen. Come, Lord Jesus!
>
> The grace of the Lord Jesus be with all the saints. Amen. (Revelation 22:20–21)

And in doing so John shows us that Revelation is not just a fantastic vision or an epic story but an invitation to a relationship, an invitation to a wedding! May our response to this invitation always be "Amen."

NOTES

•

•

•

•

•

Chapter One: The Vision of Jesus and the Letters to the Churches: Seeing the Lord Who Was Already There

1. Pope Benedict XVI, Address to U.S. Bishops, April 16, 2008, in Lachlan T. Cameron, Richard G. Henning, and Peter Vaccari, *Pope Benedict XVI's Apostolic Journey to the United States and Visit to the United Nations, April 15–20, 2008* (Strasbourg, France: Éditions du Signe, 2008), p. 121.

2. Cameron, Henning, and Vaccari, p. 124.

3. Cameron, Henning, and Vaccari, p. 121. See also Pope Benedict XVI, *Spe Salvi*, Encyclical on Christian Hope, November 30, 2007, 31, available at: www.vatican.va.

4. Cameron, Henning, and Vaccari, p. 122.

Chapter Two: The Throne of the Three, the Proclamation of the Four, and the Worship of the Twenty-Four

1. See Luigi Giussani, *The Religious Sense*, John Zucchi, trans. (Montreal: McGill-Queen's University Press, 1997).

2. Plato, *Phaedo*, 85c, in *The Republic and Other Works by Plato*, B. Jowett, trans. (Garden City, N.Y.: Anchor, 1973), p. 519, emphasis added.

3. Cardinal Roger M. Mahony, "Reflection: The Pope's Pastoral Visit, *The Tidings*, April 25, 2008, available at: www.the-tidings.com.

Chapter Three: The Seven Seals: Jesus Is Present in the Mess of History

1. Pope John Paul II, *Redemptor Hominis*, Encyclical on the Redeemer of Man, 1 (Boston: Daughters of St. Paul, 1979), pp. 5, 6.
2. See Tom Brokaw, *The Greatest Generation* (New York: Random House, 2004).
3. Quoted in *"This Is the Victory That Conquers the World, Our Faith: Exercises of the Fraternity of Communion and Liberation*, Sheila Beatty, trans. (Milan: Rimini, 2008), p. 6.

Chapter Four: The Old and the New: The Plagues, the Two Witnesses, the Ark of the Covenant, and the Woman

1. See Pope Benedict XVI, *Jesus of Nazareth: From the Baptism in the Jordan to the Transfiguration* (New York: Doubleday, 2007), chap. 1.
2. The Preface for the Feast of the Transfiguration (August 6) includes, "Jesus Christ our Lord ... revealed his glory to the disciples to strengthen them for the scandal of the cross." *New St. Joseph Weekday Missal, Vol. 2: Pentecost to Advent* (New Jersey: Catholic Book, 2002), p. 515.
3. Letter of his Holiness Pope Benedict XVI to the Bishops of the Catholic Church Concerning the Remission of the Excommunication of the Four Bishops Consecrated by Archbishop Lefebvre, March 10, 2009, available at: www.vatican.va.

Chapter Six: Love Versus Power

1. Pliny, *Letters* 10.96–97, Pliny to the Emperor Trajan, available at: www9.georgetown.edu.
2. Pliny to the Emperor Trajan.

3. See Pope Benedict XVI, *Deus Caritas Est*, Encyclical on Christian Love, December 25, 2005, www.vatican.va.

4. Address of Pope John Paul II to the Members of the John Paul II Institute for Studies on Marriage and Family, May 31, 2001, no. 3, available at: www.johnpaulii.edu.

5. See Pope John Paul II, *Love and Responsibility*, H.T. Willetts, trans. (San Francisco: Ignatius, 1993).

6. See Luigi Guissani, *At the Origin of the Christian Claim*, Vivianne Hewitt, trans.   (Montreal: McGill-Queen's University Press, 1998), pp. 71, 78.

Chapter Seven: Babylon the Harlot and Jerusalem the Bride

1. See Augustine, *Confessions*, bk. 1.

2. See J.P. Migne, ed., *Patrologia Latina* (1861), vol. 45, col. 1202, s.v. *Contra Iulianum, Opus Imperfectum, Liber Secundus*, CXLVI.

Chapter Eight: The Final Victory: The Marriage of Jesus and His Church

1. T.S. Eliot, "Choruses From 'The Rock' VI," in *The Complete Poems and Plays* (New York: Harcourt Brace, 1980), p. 106.

2. See Donal McIlraith, *Everyone's Apocalypse: A Reflection Guide* (Suva, Fiji: Pacific Regional Seminary, 1995), p. 96.

3. Giussani, p. 57.

Fr. Richard Veras is the pastor of St. Rita Church, Staten Island, New York, and the author of *Jesus of Israel: Finding Christ in the Old Testament.* He is a priest of the Archdiocese of New York, an active member of the Catholic lay movement Communion and Liberation, and a frequent contributor to *Magnificat* magazine.